JAMES
I WAS BLIND
BUT NOW I SEE
ALTUCHER

James Altucher
I WAS BLIND BUT NOW I SEE

ISBN-13: 978-1466347953
ISBN-10: 1466347953

www.jamesaltucher.com

Design, Layout, and Typesetting by Alexander Becker
www.alexanderbecker.net

Contents

Dedication

To Claudia,

My Muse

Acknowledgments

One thing I learned after six books is to keep the acknowledgments very short and specifically mention only people who helped on the book. Otherwise it's a mess and I always forget people.

So,

Claudia Azula Altucher helped edit almost every draft of the book and provided invaluable suggestions, wrote passages, and really helped me question my motives and inspiration on every sentence and chapter. She always keeps me real.

Alexander Becker put the book together: editing, formatting, cover, was proactive on suggestions to improve the content and did an excellent job. I'm really grateful for his help on this and he was a good, quick teacher explaining everything he was doing in real-time.

Dan Kelly was always good, as usual, to bounce ideas off of and take care of business while I was off writing.

My two kids, Josie and Mollie, annoyed the hell out of me while I was trying to get this book done. I know Josie is only 12 and Mollie is 9 but can't you guys drive yourselves yet to pick up your own apple turnovers? Why do I have to do that? That said, I would never have learned hula hooping without the two of you and I would have never learned what the beginnings of true love was without having two truly loveable daughters. I love you.

About The Author

James Altucher has failed at numerous businesses and careers and succeeded at a few of them. Has loved and lost and loved again. Has tried over and over to... [insert just about anything from chess to poker to hula hooping to massive lifestyle experimentation]. Has won success and lost it and occasionally wins it again. Has been on a quest for the meaning of happiness since the age of six (only because before that happiness was fairly easy and simple). Has written six prior books including *"How To Be the Luckiest Person Alive."*

Writes at the blog jamesaltucher.com the most personal, embarassing stuff a person can possibly write. Tweets at @jaltucher.

I Was Blind But Now I See

When I was six years old about half my first grade class was Jewish and about half were Christian. I was born and raised Jewish. As part of that, we always learned (through friends, school, family, etc.) jokes about Jesus. Similarly, the Christians had jokes about the Jews. We would whisper these jokes amongst ourselves but occasionally some would get out. I remember one time at lunch we had all just about had it.

It was time to fight.

Jews versus Christians.

At lunchtime we were all running around, pushing each other down to the ground, throwing dirt on each other and shoving each other. Nobody got really hurt.

Finally one kid yelled, "Wait!" And we all sort of stopped and looked at him. "Wasn't Jesus Jewish?"

Someone else said, "Yeah!"

The first kid said, "How about we compromise for the Jews to just agree that Jesus was a great teacher and then we don't have to fight."

And then after that we didn't fight.

But why would six-year-olds care enough about something 2000 years old to fight about it? It's because from an early age on, we're brainwashed about almost every single belief we hold dear.

I've believed in so much that it has ruined me. For example: I believed that marriage would lead to a happy life. That $100 million in the bank would make me happy. That going to a great college and graduate school would make me happy. That having a TV show would make me happy. The becoming a chess master would make me happy. That having a lot of sex would make me happy.

The list goes on and on of the things I thought that would make me happy. Each of the above, and 100 things more, made me so desperately unhappy at different points and yet I still fought for them, fought to control what I couldn't have in a world where I became desperately needy for everything I couldn't have.

Happiness starts when we have the freedom to pursue what's inside ourselves instead of the myriad joys and pursuits and successes that are outside ourselves.

How do we find out what happiness means so we can start to really pursue it? I describe "THE DAILY PRACTICE" in my last book and also in this book. In this book I provide much more material on it. I provide modifications and more descriptions to make it flow more smoothly depending on how much time one has to commit to it and also to explain it even more deeply than I have done before.

This practice and the techniques used in this book have worked for me. I have been able to come back from the dead. To live with my fears, to conquer my anxieties (most of the time – every day is a process), and to continue striving for success and happiness. Note I didn't say I "found" success and happiness. It's a process that continues every day. And tomorrow when I wake up again I have to apply these principles again. But every day I move closer... to what? That's it. Just closer.

WHY HAVE I BEEN WRITING THE BLOG AT JAMESALTUCHER.COM?

I want to show what a fool I've been: in business, in dating, in sex, in marriage, in fatherhood, in friendship. AND NOT JUST ONCE. Many times I've ended up broke and lonely and lost. So lost I've had to simply give up all hope of finding my way back or I would've gone completely insane.

I've also been writing this blog with a tiny bit of sleight of hand. Often when I write about the *Nine Obstacles of Success* (as an example) I'm not necessarily equating Success with money.

Money is an important step towards happiness because it buys our freedom. But when I write about creativity or how to eat what you kill, it's not only because I want you and I to have a lot of money (and we will as we follow those chapters) but to have freedom, to break down the brainwashing that chains us, and ultimately to find some happiness. Money doesn't bring happiness. But it allows us to spend more of our waking hours pursuing happiness once we have it. It's only a step towards happiness.

I've stated before but will state again, MY ONLY GOAL is happiness.

But first we have to figure out what happiness is? Because the brainwashing is so deep we're convinced that going to Harvard, getting a home, voting, getting married, is what leads to happiness. It is not.

We then think: getting more money, having more success, having fame, could lead to happiness.

It does not. We can still have all of these things. They certainly help get you the freedom to pursue happiness. But they are not the means. Just part of the process we will learn how to accomplish here.

So we have to build up our definition of "what is happiness." Then avoid the obstacles to that happiness.

And so, let's say then one achieves this elusive goal. The next step is to make sure it lasts more than a day. That it builds, that it enraptures us and helps us to enrapture and free the people around us.

BUT FIRST:

We have to RETRAIN OURSELVES FROM THE OUTSIDE IN. And then from the INSIDE OUT.

What does that mean?

It means take a look at the beliefs you hold dear. For instance, a belief that is hard to analyze is that "it's important to have a college degree." Or it's important to "vote." Or it becomes important who we vote for. And what they stand for. Or that some wars are "justified" while others aren't. We're taught from an early age what's important and what's not. When I say "early age" it's from so far back we can't even remember. Your false training starts when you are swimming the breast stroke down the birth canal.

For example, if you are feeling a little agitated as you hear the "importance of voting" belief challenged in the previous paragraph, or any of the other examples, if your blood is suddenly boiling or you feel the need to tell me off, then perhaps you are observing firsthand the depth of the profound conditioning. Looking in is a hard job, not for the faint of heart but rather for the warrior at heart. It takes courage.

We're exposed to over 10,000 ad and brand impressions every day. Each one of these imprints further programs the brainwashing we've been subjected to.

Break It All Down

We still have a chance to start over. To have the openness and sense of wonder and eager curiosity of a one-year-old while having a fresh mind that is not controlled by the external programming.

So our definition of happiness has to unravel like peeling away at an onion. And we're going to cry along the way. You can't help it. Getting to unveil your own beliefs is transformative. You will be different. Your parents, colleagues, friends, lovers, might not be happy about it. They may be weary of it, distrustful. You'll be the one-eyed king in the land of the blind and that will suddenly put you in an uncomfortable position with everyone who is still being brainwashed.

This is a good thing. It means more opportunities for success. For money. For better understanding of yourself and the world around you. For better opportunities for real happiness. YOU'RE BREAKING FREE. Now you have to stand alone, where previously you stood together, but this is where opportunity is created. Now you can see past the valleys, and over the horizon something beautiful and new awaits.

From then we have to rebuild the interior. The plumbing got all screwed up. We gambled our happiness that the exterior promises made by our elders, advertisers, governments, teachers, our friends, were real and fulfilling. But the tide has come in this past decade, things have changed, we are in a whole different beach and we're all standing around looking at each other naked.

So we have to think again. We have to put on new swimsuits, and learn to swim again. We do this by building the muscles that have long atrophied. The physical muscles, the emotional muscles, the mental muscles, and the spiritual muscles. We figure out new tools to light up our creativity, to fight fear, to eat what we kill. To hustle and then exchange society smarts with street smarts."

The 10 Commandments of James-ism

By the way, replace the word "JAMES" with your own name. "Claudia-Ism" or "Phil-Ism" or "Jane-Ism," or "Pierre-ism" or "Mario-ism," etc. You have to believe first in the many complex layers of yourself before beginning to subscribe to the beliefs of others. You need to get to the core of you and what you believe before you accept what others say or think. You have to stand on your own two feet, be your own teacher, your own light.

1. ACKNOWLEDGE THAT EVERY DAY OF YOUR LIFE YOU ARE BRAIN-WASHED. Just like when we were kids we believed in Santa Claus and how George Washington chopped down the cherry tree, now as adults we've been trained to believe in much more dangerous and insidious ideas. Being aware that you need to question everything is commandment number one, including, by the way, questioning what I'm saying to you right now.

   And then on top of the brainwashing we suffered in schools, from our parents, from our friends, from society, there's the 10,000 ad impressions each day that hit the periphery of our eyes and further tries to tell us what little intricacies of life will deliver goodness and happiness to us. We can't even begin to be happy until we at least acknowledge that SOME brainwashing has occurred. And the more we examine this brainwashing, the more we will see how in other ways we didn't even expect, we've been programmed like little robots.

2. WHO BRAINWASHED YOU? Parents, friends, teachers, government, media, entertainment, advertising, the edu-

cation system, the banking system, and organized religion. In that order although they are all interrelated.

It's not their fault. And there's no reason to be angry at them. They were brainwashed also. Everyone is just trying to survive the best way they know how. And there's been generations of mental programming combined with now trillions of dollars of advertising dollars that keep everyone in line. IT'S A MASSIVE RECRUITING MACHINE that tries to keep us from our true happiness by redefining happiness in various ways that are inaccurate and even harmful.

From here on in, we have to realize that the plane is going down and we have to put the oxygen mask on our own face first. The mega changes that occurred in the past 10 years turned the world upside down; we are in a different planet now, one that requires adapting, new ways of thinking, and of breathing. So get on your own mask, see how it feels. Breathe again.

3. WHAT CAN YOU DO ABOUT IT? Take one belief at a time, turn it upside down. Learn how to break down your beliefs. Be your own rebel. Take, for instance, the belief that "going to college leads to a better life." Try to understand why you believe that. Who told you that was true? What happens if someone told you the opposite "that NOT going to college would lead to a better life?" Does that thought disturb you? Why does it disturb you?

Some of these beliefs are so sacred inside of us that it really feels like punishable blasphemy to believe the opposite. I know this because I've had death threats and angry emails over almost every belief I've ever challenged on my blog (examples will follow later).

THE GOAL IS NOT NECESSARILY TO BELIEVE THE OPPOSITE OF ALL THE THINGS WE'VE BEEN PROGRAMMED TO BELIEVE, BUT TO SEPARATE OUT WHO WE ARE FROM OUR BELIEFS, SO THAT WE CAN TRULY EXAMINE THEM, SCRUTINIZE THEIR ROOTS, AND BE ABLE TO LOOK AT THEM FROM ALL 360 DEGREES INSTEAD OF JUST THE ACUTE SHARP ANGLES THAT HAVE BEEN SHOVED AT US ALMOST SINCE BIRTH.

Let's shed our labels. People want to be in the "tea party" or they want to be "environmentalists" or "demo-crats" or "republicans" or "a homeowner" or a "gradu-ate." Let's shed all labels for a little bit while we inspect them. Maybe they are all good labels to have. But there's nothing wrong with re-examining them under a new lens. It's understandable that we want to be part of the pack, the herd. The flock feels protective. But we've learned now that it is most likely a bag full of false protections.

The past decade has been such a hard decade in many ways. 9/11, the Internet bust (and tech depression), the wars, the loss of tens of millions of jobs, the housing crisis, the finan-cial crisis. We know, for instance, that the myth of corporate safety was just that – a myth. People who worked at corpo-rations for 40 years were fired without severance or ben-efit's. This happened. I don't mean to say "the only one you can rely on is yourself" because clearly the people who love us are valuable to us. But at the end of the day, happiness comes when we escape the robotic constructs built to house our beliefs and become real humans, and stand in the light.

I am also NOT advocating going it alone. Nobody can do every-thing alone. That is not only arrogant it is plain dangerous. But examining our own beliefs gives us a solid ground from where to relate to others in a more honest way, and create more effec-tive relationships that provide better results in the new environ-ment we find ourselves in. Honesty with yourself is the first step towards challenging the beliefs of the mega-system.

4. HAPPINESS IS THE ONLY GOAL. We don't have to know what happiness is yet. But we know this: we don't want to be sad or fearful anymore. We don't want to be anxious. We don't want to do things that cause us to feel guilt. That's a start.

THINK ABOUT IT, WHEN YOU SAY YOU WANT TO HAVE MORE MONEY, WHY IS THAT? You may answer that you want it so that you would be able to travel some more, or have more time for your children. And why is that? You may say because then you would see the world and write that novel you always wanted to write, or teach your kid to throw ball. And why is that? And you may say, because then I will be happy. So why not go for "happy" in the first place? Why the long route when there is a shortcut? Certainly money buys some degree of freedom. So getting more money is a reasonable goal. And we'll get it. But let's cut out as many intermediaries to happiness as possible.

5. THE OBSTACLES OF HAPPINESS ARE SICKNESS, INERTIA, DOUBTS, LAZINESS, CARELESSNESS, VACILLATING, LACK OF PROGRESS, DE-LUSIONS, AND FALLING BACKWARDS. Each of those allows us to fall back into our brainwashing and stop ourselves from challenging the world around us so we can break down our thoughts and see things as they truly are.

6. THE PATH TO HAPPINESS INVOLVES BEING AS HEALTHY AS WE CAN: PHYSICALLY, EMOTIONALLY, MENTALLY, AND SPIRITUALLY.

7. PHYSICALLY: We can exercise, we can try to eat healthy, we can sleep eight hours, we can avoid alcohol and other foods or liquids that are either hard to digest or will later inhibit the brain cells we desperately need to enjoy quality of life in our elder years. This is hard. I'm not advocating being a vegan, or a weight lifter, or a yogi. Just being aware. When I was younger I could eat five Big Macs a day. Now if I eat more than two meals a day it becomes much harder for me to digest and clean my system. I'm 43. It's important for me to make sure when I'm 83 I'm still healthy and able to explore the things that make me really happy. The root of almost all physical ailments as we age is what we put into our intestines (and lungs).

8. EMOTIONALLY: I'm a pretty angry guy. I feel a lot of peo-ple have wronged me and, it's not just a feeling – a lot of people have wronged me. I also have a lot of regrets. A lot of things have happened to me that are my fault that still make me sad. But dwelling on this does neither me nor them any good. You can't be healthy if you obsess on the crappy people or events in your life. More on that later.

Also, fear is an important topic here. We try so hard to control the world around us. Will it give us money? Will it get us the girl? Will it get us the job we want or the promotion we want or will it get us the customers and allow us to build the business we want? These are just a few of the things I often wake up first thing in the morning afraid about. Fear gets in the way of finding out what makes us happy. You can't be happy if you're stressed. Controlling the world and have it going your way will only lead to a temporary happiness. What happens the next time the world goes a different way? Then you aren't happy anymore.

9. Mentally: Your mind needs to be as sharp and creative as possible. You need this for two reasons. One is so you are creative enough to achieve the success and money that will allow you to pursue and purchase your freedom. Two so that you can train the analytical parts of your mind to break down all the myths that we hold true every day. I have several chapters on this.

10. Spiritually: This word has a bad connotation. It sort of smells "new age-y." Or like organized religion, which many people despise and have rebelled against. But what I really mean is "Surrender." If you wanted the Earth to move out of its orbit from the Sun, you would give up. You can't do it. You would try (somehow, I don't even know how you would try) and then finally you'd say, "I give up. I can't do it." In general, life is like that. We have dreams, most of them don't work out, and we can either continue to force those dreams into place, or we can give up. Giving up doesn't have to be a sad thing. It's a transition. It's a little death (a term often used to describe an orgasm).

Sometimes you're just on the floor, failure has slashed you again, and all you can do is look up at the sky and say, "You win. I give up. Tell me what you want me to do and I'll do it." And you hand yourself over.

To who? Not to God. Not to an old man with a beard living up in the sky. But deep inside you there is a creative force that desperately wants you to succeed, wants you to make a lot of money, wants you to fall in love and be happy, wants you to do these things not so you can live in exotic mansions and travel the world fifty times over, but so that you are free from the constraints of a normal job and can pursue the real exploration of what and where is the happiness around you.

Follow these ten ideas with discipline (described more throughout the book) and you will make more money than you know what to do with. This world is filled with money. The global economy is over $50 trillion dollars. You only need a tiny speck of that to have the freedom to quit your nine to five job where you are totally exploited, so that you can then take a breather, live a long healthy life, and pursue the things that really make you happy.

If you are just a little more creative, emotionally healthy, and physically healthy, than your competition and you avoid the nine obstacles, then that money is eventually yours. Money is the most external manifestation of the spirituality that's the tenth commandment above. It stems from the fabric of your core beliefs. Smart and strong subtle beliefs lead to the clarity and efficiency that can make riches manifest.

Follow these ten ideas and you will start to have the relationships that bring you up instead of down. You will have the creativity to bounce from idea to idea to explore what's real in your brainwashing and what isn't. Ultimately, you'll change and you'll change from being robot to a human, from a zombie to truly alive.

You'll look around and see all of the zombies with the glazed look in their eyes, their angry anonymous thoughts flaring through their heads, their desperation and neediness for more money, more sex, more of anything that will make them forget what their real goal is

For everyone of us that clicks and comes to "know thyself" a thousand others follow. The zombies can see the light once you become the beacon. Everything that was a zombie in you will shed away, like the bandages that covered the mummy, until finally a real human will stand up. Others will notice, some may hate you, some will be curious; some of us will get back to swimming happily in the new ocean.

That human will look straight at the sun for the first time with eyes uncovered by bandages. And the sun will be so happy to see you she will smile right back.

What is This Book?

This book is divided into two parts. First, looking at the ways in which the mega-recruitment machines have hypnotized us into believing what they wanted us to believe: so they could take our money, fight wars, convince us that we were safe while they took advantage of our hard work in exchange for that myth of protection.

I bring these things up not to convince you that they were all WRONG. I could care less what they were.

Nothing I say in this book will change anything that happens on the outside. Wars will still be fought. The recruitment machines, funded by billions of dollars, will continue to run their assembly lines of zombie creation. You and I can't stop that. Fighting with a pig only makes you muddy and the pig happy.

But I bring them up to show how looking at the beliefs we hold dear can be examined under a microscope, and perhaps even modified inside of ourselves so they don't have as large an effect (e.g. they stop taking our money so we can use that money for other means – like buying our freedom and pursuing more individual dreams instead of the pre-boxed sets that they so beautifully wrapped up for us).

That's Part One.

Part Two is WHEN WE GET INTO THE NITTY GRITTY OF WHAT HAPPINESS REALLY IS and how can we find it. Two sources try to tell us what happiness is:

The 10,000 ad impressions we get each day which try to convince us what shaving cream, what potato chip, what college, what mortgage rate, what charity, will make us happier.

The monolith of the self-help industry. Whether it's "positive thinking" or "pain bodies" or the "law of attraction" or "optimism diets," none of that will ultimately work. Words are just words. Even this book won't do anything for anyone without hard practice and work. We want to be happy so we fork over our dollars to these industries.

But at the end of the day we are all primarily householders. We don't have time to meditate for three hours and then do yoga and then do neurolinguistic programming and self-hypnosis while we diet.

We have families to raise. We have careers to pursue. We have money to make. We have colleagues and family to deal with. We have real fears that invade us at night. I have real fears. Things I'm scared of every single day. It's only through diligent work that we can start to overcome these fears. With fear comes stress, and stress leads to sickness, inertia, and all of the other things that slows down our happiness.

And sometimes we can't just wake up at 5:30am and go to sleep at 8pm (as I suggest in my prior book) and write down 10 ideas a day. Sometimes we need to give ourselves a break and modify things until times and schedules permit. I'll discuss this more in part two by giving different exercises and modifications to the Daily Practice. How to deal with the people who bring us down, how to fight the fear, how to be creative – these are all components of bringing a daily practice into your life so that not only does your entire life change, it changes so quickly that you won't even recognize the final result.

PART I
I WAS BLIND...

The 10 Commandments of The American Religion

Look at some of the external beliefs we hold dear and break them down. I'm not saying you should agree or disagree with me. Let's just look at these commonly held beliefs from a different viewpoint. Let's learn how to look at things upside down. Upside down, backwards and forwards, let's tear these little issues apart and we'll see who is naked in the ocean when the tide comes in.

Let's start with the most external. When I say the "ten commandments" of the American religion, I'm obviously making it up. There aren't any commandments. There is no American Religion. But this is an exercise in seeing some of the ideas we've been programmed with almost from birth.

Let's take a look at these ideas and see how truly bad it feels to look at the opposite of these beliefs.

If I stand in the center of Times Square, New York City, and said something like *"Moses didn't part the Red Sea"* or *"Jesus never existed"* everyone would just keep walking around me, ignoring what I said, etc. Whatever, they would be thinking: I have things to do, very important things that have to get done. And this guy is clearly crazy so not worth my time.

But if I stood there and said, *"going to college is the worst sin you can force your kids to commit,"* or *"you should never vote again"* or *"World War II was not a holy war"* or *"never own a home again,"* I would probably be lynched on the spot.

The American Religion is a fickle and false religion. Used to replace the ideologies we (a country of immigrants) escaped from with tenets that don't withstand the test of time. With random high priests lurking all over the Internet, ready to pounce. Below are some of the tenets of the American Religion.

A strong belief in any of the below will lead you to want to control the world so that it provides these things for you. Not getting these things will lead to fear. Fear leads to stress, unhappiness, and feelings of lack of control over our lives that won't go away.

There's that book, "The Law of Attraction" which says that if you autosuggest you want a "home" then you will attract it. The Law of Attraction is BS. When you fully break down the misbeliefs and disbeliefs that have diseased your mind and spirit then the right things will be attracted to you. There are no Laws. You become the Law.

You will have the health in every way, the creativity in every way, the ability to fight your fears inside of you and outside of you that make you a nation unto yourself. Nations make their own laws.

There are more than these ten things. There are one thousand commandments to the American Religion. But this is a decent start.

Commandment #1: The Frontier

My kid has to read about "Lewis and Clark" this summer as she prepares to go into the fourth grade. The "frontier" is a very beautiful, almost spiritual concept. The idea that we can always expand, always improve. For the first several hundred years after the Europeans took over the United States we expanded into every unmapped territory and killed everyone in our path.

The frontier represented this spiritual mystery – a physical manifestation of the unknown. An escape. An escape from the debt collectors, from our families, from the government and it's rules. The frontier was dangerous but there was the promise (or hope) of wealth, of happiness. So we left, we conquered the frontier.

But then what's on the other side?

WHAT WENT WRONG WITH THE FRONTIER?

We're missing out on the more subtle points of the word "Frontier." For the past several decades we've expanded into the frontier of technology, creating everything from computers, to rockets that go to the moon, to the Internet, and many cures for many diseases (polio, smallpox, etc). This is exciting, what the spirit of America is all about.

But now our innovators, technologists, and creators have to pay down their homeowner debt, their credit card debt, and their student loan debt. They have to vote for people who never truly represent them and get us further and further into trouble. The government puts more and more hurdles in front of our creators. The frontier needs to go into another direction. It sounds "new age" to say the frontier needs to go inwards. But clearly, the hope for an escape, for more, for danger, for a different kind of wealth and success, needs to take a drastically different and creative direction in order for us to truly conquer a new frontier, since it's not the obvious.

Who knows what further twists and warps the American Religion will take to destroy us more than we've already been destroyed? At the end of the physical frontier is the ocean, and we're all being pushed into it until America and everyone in it drowns.

Commandment #2: Own A Home

The American Religion wants you to have a home with a white picket fence. Why would the high priests of the American religion want that?

So then you owe the banks money for 30 years or more (after second, third, fourth mortgages). The banks need to borrow from your checking account at 0.5% and then lend right back to you at 8%. That's how they make money and it's one of the largest industries in the country.

So you are not flexible as to where you can move. The job market is ruled by supply and demand. Supply of jobs in an area is finite. So they want to make sure you can't move so quickly so that demand only goes up (you can't move and more and more people hit the age of 18 or higher).

Note that many people equate owning a home with "having roots." It's as if owning a home connects you in some immortal way with the 3 billion year old planet. Your roots are now connected to it.

It's linking "home ownership" with the delusion of immortality, the "fear of death" that every religion attempts to assuage (through "heaven," "reincarnation," etc.)

See the below chapter to read more about *Why I Would Rather Shoot Myself in the Head than Ever Own a Home Again.*

Commandment #3: Go To College

There's the myth that going to college leads to "a better life" or a "promised future." Almost like how the contract Abraham had with God would lead to Judaism being a group of "chosen people." A couple of points:

Statistically, there's no proof that smart, ambitious, aggressive people, won't benefit enormously from a five year head start against their peers who choose to spend five years doing homework and drinking beer and going to frat parties. (Don't quote me the statistic about the differences in salaries between college grads and non-college grads, because there's enormous selection bias in that statistic and it's like comparing apples and oranges right now).

The government needs to pay off $74 trillion in Social Security in the next 50 years. They have to make money somehow so student loan debt is now higher than credit card debt for the first time in 50 years. Imagine that. We send our young, fresh, children off to college and then 5 years later (5 years is average time spent in college by those who GRADUATE) they come out owing the government $100,000+. Thank god the government gets to exploit our kids so they can pay off the promises they made under Lyndon Johnson during the Vietnam War.

There are so many exciting alternatives to college. I list some of them in my last book, *"How to Be the Luckiest Person Alive".* I'm excited for my children, because I hope they have experiences that will teach them to stand on their feet, get to see the world early, realize their deepest dreams, live a life of wonder, be grounded yet creative, learn to eat what they kill. I much rather they experience this rather than sending them into the rat race so they can end up ignorant, in debt, and working at nonsense jobs so they can pay off the gangsters who have guns pointed right at their heads.

One anecdote: the guy who caught Derek Jeter's 3000th hit. He was a young man in the stadium. He's a salesclerk at Verizon. I have nothing against that job. Anyone can do what they want. But he also has $150,000 in student loans to pay back. Why couldn't he get a better job with his college degree? Why did he just give Jeter his ball back? Jeter is going to make $100 million in the next few years. This guy could've paid his loans back and been free. FREEDOM is everything. He wanted to be a "good guy."

The American Religion needs you to be in debt. Needs you to pay hundreds of thousands of dollars to read the same Plato you could've read in the bathroom at your local library. "You'll have a better life." "Life is secure now." Yes, you are fully secured by the shackles they hand you on graduation day.

See below: "FAQ on Not Going to College" where I answer some of the questions that were posed to me after my initial articles on this topic.

What about employees who will NOT hire people without college degrees? And my answer would be: Who needs them? Innovation and better raising of our children can leave them better standing in this new world. Don't work for small-minded people or you become small-minded.

Commandment #4: Holy Wars

Apparently some wars are "holy" and can't be argued against.

I disagree with this but that's my opinion. When I try to state that opinion I get everyone coming out of the woodwork wanting to argue obscure history with me. At the end of the day, any excuse to kill little children is not an excuse I can believe in.

All I want is to prevent 18 year old kids (and younger) from dying. Even without a Draft, no 18-year-old willingly signs up to die. Or to have his legs blown off. And, in most cases, the judgment of history is centuries away from deciding what wars were "correct" wars or not. We'll all be dead by the time those decisions are made for us.

That's the basis of my argument. We can argue all the history we want after that. No matter what the war is, I will never send my 18 year olds off to war. I'd rather go in their place if there was a forced draft.

We can all agree Vietnam was no good. Korea was probably no good. Iraq was no good. But are other wars "holy" and justified? When other countries (UK, for instance) released their slaves in 1833 we had to fight a war to release our slaves. And note that the slaves weren't released until 1862, when Lincoln, who couldn't care less about them, was afraid we were going to lose the Civil War, a war fought over whether or not the North could still control the tariffs of the Southern cotton when the Southern states seceded (as was their right). And if we had never fought the Revolutionary War (a war fought over Sam Adams' taxes) Britain would've set aside money to buy out all of the US slaves in 1833. Both wars were senseless. What about WWII? Time magazine named Hitler "Man of the Year" in 1938. What a bunch of fools we were and still are. We could've stopped him economically as soon as his vile persecutions began but we turned away thinking he would stop Stalin. Stalin murdered 50 million people while we did nothing.

No matter what the argument is: don't send 18 year old children to their death. Even if you think I'm dead wrong. The nuclear attacks on little babies were no good. If you want to fight a war, go yourself and fight it, or be willing to admit you would fight it at the age of 40.

Commandment #5: The U.S. Constitution

There's no document more sacred (as it should be) in the American Religion. And yet, just like the principles of the Bible are often forgotten by its highest adherents, ditto goes twice over for the U.S. Constitution. For instance, who has the power to declare war? Congress does, according to the Constitution. The House hasn't declared war on anyone since 1941. The U.S. Constitution is HOLY, HOLY, HOLY in the American Religion until those moments when we break the rules. Then everyone looks the other way. "We had to do it that way to protect our way of life," is the common refrain.

Someone is always protecting me and my way of life. I'm fine thank you.

Commandment #6: Charity

Because the American Religion, unlike most religions, doesn't have a strict code of ethics, giving to charity is often considered the sign of a "good person." A couple of points on that:

Giving to charity costs money. So the best people in the American Religion then, are the ones who have the most money to give.

Volunteering is more and more difficult for people who have to pay back student loans and exorbitant home loans. Good luck volunteering when your children need to be fed or when you are an indentured servant, thanks to your advanced learning in the ivory tower.

Let's go over the math of every dollar you spend on charity. When you give $100 to a major charity, most of that goes into the bank. They then invest the money. On the interest they make on their investments, a percentage of that money goes to actual charity, another percentage goes to salaries. So for every dollar you give to charity, about 2 cents a year, give or take, goes to the actual charitable cause you wanted to support. Now let's break that down even further. How many charities have executives making over $500,000 a year? A lot. And let's say it's a medical charity. Now most of the money is going towards drugs that cost billions of dollars to approve. See the next point.

Of course not all charities are evil. Many are trying to do good. But blindly donating or volunteering to one doesn't make it good.

Commandment #7: The Food & Drug Administration

What is this organization? Is it in the Constitution? Does it do any good? The FDA requires that drugs go through trials to prove their safety and effectiveness. That sounds good, right? Before you give an 80 year old man a drug for cancer let's make sure it doesn't kill him. Meanwhile let's send 18 year olds off to wars that the House/ Constitution hasn't approved of since 1941.

It costs billions of dollars to build those trials and the FDA can shut you down at any point. Companies raise those billions from charities and from individual investors, who usually lose all of their money when the FDA shuts down a trial. But what's the solution?

Well, we have the Internet now. We have social media. We have "word of mouth" on steroids. That's what technology and innovation is for. Let's expand the frontier, let's get the drugs out there. We can all see which scientists worked on them and what their backgrounds are; we can all read the patents; we can read real-life experiences from people using the drug.

The Internet will conduct "virtual trials." Will people die? Yes, but people die in FDA trials anyway. Will more lives be saved? Of course! Many drug companies just give up (they can't raise the money even if their drugs are miracle drugs). Now they can get those drugs out there and we can really see. I want the FDA out of my body and let me ingest whatever I want, particularly if I have a terminal disease.

Commandment #8: Stocks

I'm bullish from birth on stocks. I think the American economy will do well, we will continue to innovate, and the creators and innovators (particularly the ones who manage to avoid being held captive by the American Religion) will continue to build successful businesses.

So I do think stocks in the long haul will continue to go up. However, in the reasons I outline in the chapter below, I do not think the best way for you to make money is to own stocks. Much better is to be creative. To start your own business. To light your own fire that people follow when the darkness becomes unbearable.

Too many people are eager to say it's over or that *"the banks have stolen everything from us."* Let me tell you an immutable fact: the global economy is $50 trillion dollars. If you avoid the obstacles that stand in your path (discussed below), if you find the persistence to build up the muscles (physical, emotional, mental, and spiritual, discussed in part two) then will join the army of people who rise up and take the pieces of that $50 trillion dollar economy that they rightly deserve. It doesn't matter if we are in a Depression, a war, a bad President, etc. None of that matters.

But stocks are rigged. I've seen it too many times I've seen the rigging happen right in front of me. It's not the path to wealth.

Commandment #9: Money And Success

We need money to survive. To feed our families. To accumulate freedom for ourselves. Freedom for what? Not to pursue base pleasures on a yacht in the middle of the ocean. But to find the time to explore ourselves and find out what we stand for, what we mean, who we are, where we came from, in the limited time we've been given here. Life is a gift. The fact that we live in such a wondrous time where freedom can be acquired through various means is an unbelievable spiritual gift that allows us to go deeper than the generations before us.

I'm not talking about "religion" since that has become a twisted word (not a bad word, but unfortunately it's a word that many rebel from). We have thoughts that run all day in our head. Where are those thoughts coming from? Could we be happier if we tweak those thoughts? Could we, dare I say it, be healthier if those thoughts are happier. It's not easy to be happy. Many billionaires are desperately unhappy.

But in America today, to strive for more and more has become part of our religion. To be envious (and I am guilty of this) of those who have more than us, is a disease. We confuse happiness with the fame, fortune, and often respect that success brings.

Everything in this book is about preparation. Not preparation to be a great entrepreneur. Or to be an intellectual against the belief system we've been programmed with, but preparation to be a real human, above the animals and robots that walk around us every day, mindless in their thoughts of domination, of anger, of greed, of fear.

To be prepared we have to be healthy. We have to be ready to receive the money that is waiting for us. And then use that money to pay the ticket-master for our freedom. Freedom to choose the "enough" show so that we can devote the resources of our health and money to better ourselves and learn and live as much as we can before the tiny flickering candle that is our life melts and fades to black.

Commandment #10: The Media Is The "Fourth Branch"

There's this weird idea that's developed over the past fifty years (encouraged by the success of Robert Redford playing Bob Woodward in "All The President's Men") that the media is somehow a "check" on the other three branches of government. This is ridiculous, but people still don't get it.

A few months ago everyone was getting panicked that radiation from Japan was going to get washed up on the shores of San Francisco. Did that happen? Of course not. But the media doesn't apologize for the thousands of people who got sick taking iodine pills, or who spent weeks away from supposedly radioactive areas.

Then there was the whole "debt ceiling scare" and "will America default". Every week there is a new fear. Will "bird flu" turn into "swine flu" turn into, I don't know, "cat flu" or something horrible and gross. Will Greece debt (a country with the GDP of Connecticut) somehow spread like a "contagion" across the Atlantic into the United States? And when there's nothing to worry about that week we get the usual annual stories they store up way in advance: "America's Obesity Problem," "Divorced Kids Are Ruined," etc. And whatever happened to all those "crack babies." Aren't they supposed to be all grown up now? Terrorizing the country? Where did that 20 year old fear story go? And yet, crime is at an all-time low in America.

I obviously don't think the media should be shut down. But there certainly should be a greater sense of responsibility than simply scaring the hell out of people with a new topic every single week. I am so bored of the "fear of the week." I'd rather watch *Snooki* all day long than another "fear of the week" analysis from the pseudo-experts who are desperate for screen time. I know these people. They are whores for screen time. They will say anything. One time a show booker called me and said, "Do you believe in X?" She wanted me to fight for X because they found someone who would fight

34

for the opposite of X. I said, "Yeah, I strongly believe in X!" An hour later she called me back and said, "We lost our anti-X guy. Can you argue for anti-X?"

Didn't she hear me? I said, *"I strongly believe in X!"* Guess what, I still went on and considered that anti-X might be valid. You can blame me. This was years ago and I've made far worse mistakes with my life and with my family and friends and homes and money. This was the least important of my mistakes. But I'm telling you this because this is how the media works. Know it, and use it as a tool instead of you being the tool.

The best thing you can do is avoid all news. Let's look at a few key issues. First off, what are my qualifications here? I've worked for over a dozen media companies. I've written for newspaper, TV shows, I've been a pundit on TV shows, I'm the worst culprit. So I know what they are up to.

Another time I was backstage at a news show. The news show had the latest on various disasters, economic fear, stocks going down, governments rebelling, etc. The producer leaned over to me and said: *"Don't fool yourself – all of this is just filler in between advertisements."*

In other words, the media thinks you are an idiot. And I don't blame them. They have families to feed also. And it's not a crime to tell you a white lie on TV. Or to make you a little scared. Or a little greedy. For some people that's entertainment.

But nothing you read in the paper today will make you happier (well, I'm legitimately happy when I see wedding photos of Kim Kardashian's wedding but we'll give that a pass).

Every week, a newsroom gets all of their best reporters and editors together on a Monday morning. Then the top guy says, *"Ok, what have you got?"* And the reporters have to respond with items that are designed to induce more and more terror. When the top guy thinks the terror is sufficient to beat out the competition he says, *"Ok, let's go with it."*

And that's how news is created. Not to inform you but to scare you.

What Beliefs Are True, What Beliefs Are False?

I LOVE THIS COUNTRY. BUT I GET SAD WHEN I SEE ALL OF THE ABOVE. WHEN 18-YEAR-OLDS ARE SENT TO GET KILLED while 60-year-olds can't get the drugs they need to survive. When we follow a rusty old paradigm where the government and banks and even charities take all my money. Where commercialism, in its worst form, conspires to take the remaining dollars of my salary.

I'M NOT POLITICAL. I'm not in any party nor do I believe in any political philosophy. Fighting for a political philosophy is like masturbating straight into the hole of the bathroom wall.

For me, I believe in the impossible. That change, even at a mass level, only comes from the inside of each individual. THAT IF EACH PERSON TRIES TO REMAIN PHYSICALLY HEALTHY, EMOTIONALLY HEALTHY, MENTALLY HEALTHY, AND SPIRITUALLY HEALTHY, THEN THE COUNTRY ITSELF WILL RISE TO NEW HEIGHTS never seen before in the civilization of man: a height without delusions, without fantasy notions of a "better life" that turn out to be just lies, without deeper and more complicated mechanisms to control the masses, and where mediocrity is not rewarded with power over the creators.

A country where every individual uses her own internal compass to make decisions and flourishes in spite of marketing machines, where each of us makes decisions based on whether or not they align with our own internal new frontiers that promote innovation and personal growth of the real kind, the one that makes us happy to wake up in the morning because we know we are going to be doing what we love.

Some of the items mentioned above I'm going to look at more closely in the chapters below. And then, in Part Two, I'm going to focus on how to build up the internal. *How to truly become a human again. How to eat what you kill. How to light your creativity on fire,* and *how you can find happiness from the inside out.* Then the universe will deliver itself to you and you become the master instead of the robot.

Today I'm going to do what I always do. And it has nothing to do with anything in this section of the book. I am going to wisely ignore all the commandments.

College

Here's a trick: write the same controversial article every year. Here's where I've written articles about why kids should not go to college:

- In the Financial Times in 2005. Yes, I was the first to bring up this idea.

- In the Wall Street Journal

- In thestreet.com

- In my book, "The Forever Portfolio"

- On Yahoo Finance. Three times.

- In Business Insider

- The Washington Post

- New York Magazine (someone else wrote that one. But I was quoted heavily)

- NPR

- In the Huffington Post. And the exact same article in the NY Post. Can you imagine that? HuffPo AND the NY Post. I might not even have changed a word.

And now, finally, people are listening. But people don't like it. In a chapter below I share a death threat I received after writing one of these articles. People are very angry if you touch their hard-core beliefs.

We don't need a college education to have a better, happier life. People are starting to listen and realize it's been a scam for at least the last 15 years. Maybe 25 years.

I hate to admit it, but I don't really like anyone to disagree with me. I like 100% agreement to all of my proclamations. When I wake up in the morning, I want to open the newspaper and see big headlines, "James Altucher Was Right Again!" and quotes in the articles like, *"Why are we always so stupid? Why don't we listen to James the first time he says things?"*

Maybe when I walk outside I want people to throw flowers down on the street in front of me and beggars and homeless people to run up to me and say, *"I might be homeless but I love the way you think. If possible, can I touch you?"*

But I don't like to be touched so I would hold up my hand, take out a pad, write down some words of wisdom, rip out the piece of paper from the pad and hand it to them.

So it disturbs me when people cling to the notion of going to college like it's the holiest water down from God, come to bless them. Seriously, you could walk around and say, *"Jesus never lived,"* and people nod their heads and say, *"ok, there is religious freedom in America and what he just said is fine,"* but if you say *"kids should not go to college"* it's like you breached the highest, holiest, divine hymen of American religion.

Say it again. Say it loud and proud: *"college is the divine hymen of American religion."*

One person wrote on a Yahoo message board (where the elite post their thoughts) about me:

"The government should take his kids away." Please, that would be great for me. Maybe I can visit my kids on holidays inside their government compounds. I hear that inside the Department of Commerce there are lots of jungle gyms my kids could play on. And there are 3D video games projected onto the walls of the State Department where Chelsea Clinton's future kids will play. But until then, my kids who were taken from me by G-Force Government Agents can play the games. When Chelsea Clinton's kids are old enough, my kids can babysit them. That would help them build their rolodex for when they later on want to work at hedge funds or the world famous US Department of State.

Another person wrote:

"Mr. Altucher, who went to his prestigious Ivy League school, wants to now keep everyone underneath him so he can reap the benefits of their poverty." Yes, I admit it. I need everyone to be less educated than me so I can feel good about myself. If you didn't go to the same school as me then it's a guranlee you are less intelligent than me. As I write this I see I misspelled "guarantee" in the sentence before this one. I'm not even going to correct it. Because in the next version of the American Dictionary they will include "gurantee" and say as the definition: "see 'guarantee.'" Because that's the way I roll.

Ok, those were the spurious disagreements with my articles.

I've listed my reasons why kids shouldn't go to college on several different occasions. Let's flip it on its side. What if you didn't go to college? How great would that be?

You'd have a five year head start on all of your peers. Why five years? The average college graduate takes five years to graduate instead of four. You wouldn't have any debt. You could accumulate real world experience in any number of fields that you are interested in. For example, if you wanted to be a computer programmer, you could buy books on computer programming, study it on your own without paying the exorbitant costs of college, maybe start a company or work cheaply for a startup – in other words, get enough real world experience to be actually valuable to the society around you.

Or if you wanted to be a medical professional, you could actually work in a hospital (as anything), figure out what area of the profession really stirs up some passion in you. Read as much as possible about the profession. Understand the changing technologies. Then, with money saved up, a true passion unleashed inside of you, and a hunger to help people, you are much better equipped to make a decision. For instance, there are programs that combine bachelor's degrees with medical degrees. Too many doctors get out of 10 years of schooling still unsure what they are passionate about. What ends up happening? Bad doctors. We all know the stories. We've all lived through it. Or not lived through it.

Well, many say: *"Aren't kids socialized in college?"* I guess you can say I was socialized. I drank, tried drugs, fooled around with girls, learned how to manipulate a large bureaucratic system, and took advantage of the generosity of lenders for the first time so I could get into debt. And who did I socialize with? The exact demographic of people I socialized with for the first 18 years of my life. Middle class Jews with a smattering of everything else.

Imagine how great if I had just taken 1/10 of the money it would've cost me to go to college and really socialized. Traveled to India or China. Learned other cultures. Lived cheaply in extreme conditions. Had experiences that I wouldn't end up having for another 20 years because I was too busy paying down debt, then raising a family, then doing whatever it took to stay "successful" (which was a heavy process since I also learned the hard way what it meant to be a "failure").

Maybe I'm completely wrong. Maybe everyone should go to five years of college, get $100,000 in debt, socialize with the same demographic they've always been socializing with, take classes on Plato and Shakespeare, and learn life in the ivory tower. Maybe that's the correct path to happiness in this world. Who am I to judge?

But it's time we start looking at the opposites instead of just blindly following in the paths of the robots before us. I can rant and say we are graduating a generation of indentured servants instead of leaders, creators, and innovators, because of the massive debt loads. But I've written those articles and now we can leave these arguments to the pundit's, the TV shows, the news rags, whatever. Our only goal here is to start training the brain to consider the opposite. We want 360 degree vision. Not narrow near sightedness.

In my last book (and on my blog) I wrote a chapter *"8 alternatives to college."* One of them was "Master a Game." The idea is that some games (whether it's Ping-Pong, volleyball, chess, backgammon, poker, etc.) require massive amounts of discipline and training to get good at. And, in many cases, the training is different than what you see in the college system. So why not get good at something that very few people are good at and train your mind in a unique way as well?

But that's beside the point. Let me tell you a story: A few months ago, a woman wrote to me: *"my son has read your articles on college and is now taking a year off from going to college to pursue his passions."*

I felt a little bad. I wasn't sure why she was writing me. Maybe she was unhappy with me for playing a role in her son's decisions.

Well, I asked, *"what does your son do?"*

"He's the #1 ranking 18-year-old chess-player in the country."

Perfect! How about I take lessons from him? We settled on a price.

Last time I saw him he had just won a tournament in Norway. Now we are meeting once a week and I'm getting better at chess and he's pursuing a passion that will give him discipline, allow him to travel the world, not go into debt and maybe even make some money. Will he go to college later? Who knows? But we are living right now, not next year. And this year he will probably have a very worthwhile (and fun) year. Will it be the best year of his life so far? Actually, probably.

FAQ on Not Going to College

A lot of these questions have come up after I wrote my initial articles. Sometimes they came up in comments, sometimes in interviews, sometimes from anonymous people sending me hate-mail. I'm an equal opportunity answerer so I answer the questions below.

Q: WHAT IF SOMEONE WANTS TO BE A LAWYER? DON'T THEY NEED COLLEGE?

Do they? When I use a lawyer they usually find a file on their computer (e.g. "Generic Will"), they print it up, put my name in all the blanks, and have me sign it. Then I get charged $10,000.

There's clearly a massive arbitrage in the services lawyers provide and the costs of those services to the lawyers. This creates an opportunity that someone will eventually take advantage of.

Of course, if you want to do courtroom law, you have to buy into the scam. There's a massive recruitment machine: the judges, the other lawyers, the belief that you need to be someone who was bored out of their minds with an extra three years of schooling. That's fine. That will ultimately change.

But if you want to be a lawyer and wish to avoid the traditional route there are states that will let you take the Bar without a degree. And there are business opportunities that might allow you to participate in giving legal advice without necessarily having a law degree. Trust me when I say that paralegals often know more than the lawyers they are helping. But they don't have the degree. So they are forever shamed by the recruitment machine that perpetuates the scam.

Allow me to play with the idea a little more. Say that a bright 18 year old kid wanted to be a lawyer badly and he went to a certain state and passed the Bar by studying and taking an apprenticeship with a local law firm (some states allow that but not all). How much smarter would that kid be on day one of being a lawyer than the one that just came out of Harvard and will be sentenced to a caucus room with no windows for a minimum of a year to do "due diligence" on an average of 3000 boxes filled with useless documents, other than maybe 3, which he will have to find.

Also, the kid that went the different route will know how to say hello and thank you to his or her secretary, something that many Ivy League graduates seem to forget, notoriously on their first year, and guess what? Saying hello to secretaries opens doors.

Q: WHEN YOU SAY THAT PARENTS SHOULD NOT SEND THEIR KIDS TO COLLEGE, DO YOU MEAN THAT THEY SHOULD NOT GO TO COLLEGE INDEFINITELY? OR COME BACK TO COLLEGE LATER IN LIFE?

Kids at 18 have no idea what they want to do in life. The world is a very big place. It's bigger than five classes a day on philosophy or chemical engineering. Most kids at 18 don't relish philosophy but they relish the experience of freedom and being out of their parents' home for the first time in their lives. There is nothing wrong with this. Young adults have a lot of energy and should use it.

But the problem is that college costs have risen 1000% in the past 30 years while healthcare has risen 700% and inflation has risen "only" 300%. Colleges have made use of the myth that you can't get a job unless you have a college education. So young people feel a rush to get that college out of the way so they can get a job and "begin" their adult lives. I think kids should begin their adult lives at 18 by experiencing what else the world has to offer other than a classroom (which they've all just been locked in for the prior 18 years). A rose needs space to bloom.

Then, later, if they've thought about the debt burden they will place themselves and their parents in, they can choose to go to college. RIGHT NOW STUDENT LOAN DEBT IS GREATER THAN HOMEOWNER DEBT AND CREDIT CARD DEBT IN THIS COUNTRY. That's a lot of debt. Whereas previously we've created generations of innovators and creators, now we are creating a generation of young people mired down in hopeless debt. When will they get to live life?

Q: "OH, JAMES ALTUCHER WENT TO COLLEGE SO HE SHOULDN'T BE TALKING ABOUT THIS".

Well, why not?

The first day I was in college I saw what people were doing in college. I know now how much I learned in college and how much I learned in other experiences in life and which is more relevant to me now at the age of 43. And, by the way, it was much cheaper when I went to school than it is now.

So when did I develop this theory? Almost immediately when I realized college had nothing to do with any successes or failures that I had in life (and I had A LOT of failure despite college). And also, it took me 8 years to pay back my student loan debt. Now it takes kids 30 years to pay down that debt. It's not fair to the youth of our country.

Let's not forget the recruitment machine that has huge incentive to send you to college:

The college graduates who went before you who need validation that their own life choices were worthy.

The banking system that lends you money to go to college.

The colleges themselves that pay heavier salaries and do more construction to make your experience supposedly more worthwhile.

To summarize:

- You learn very little that you use in real life.

- You are so burdened by debt that you can't use your new-found knowledge to create real freedom and joy for yourself.

- A young person can use their energy in many other ways than just college.

Q: Do you think that nothing well worth learning is taught in college? Or is it the fact that students might not be willing to learn?

There are many things worth learning in college. And not every person in the world should avoid college. But the best colleges cost a lot of money and it's a burden for young people. And most things that you can learn in college you can learn for free outside of college thanks to the Internet. For instance, computer programming is best learned on the job. English literature is best learned by reading the books you are passionate about. Writing is best learned by having real experiences, writing every day, and reading the great writers who inspire you. Philosophy is learned by having real experiences and reading the philosophers or religious practitioners who inspire you. Imagine learning all of these things because of real world experiences, and then not having any debt. Also, when learning is not force-fed to you, you develop a real love and knowledge for how to learn on your own and that's something you keep for the rest of your life. Most young people don't learn this.

Q: Do you think you learned anything when you went to college? Or do you think you could have learned more if you chose not to go to college?

I went to college from 1986-1989. I was paying for it with debt so I graduated in 3 years. I took six courses a semester so I could graduate early. And I took courses every summer. I also worked about

30-40 hours a week at jobs so I could afford my expenses outside of tuition. Even then I graduated with enormous debt. I majored in Computer Science and learned how to program. I thought I was a very good programmer when I graduated college. I prided myself into thinking I was the best since I was sure I was better than any of my classmates. While I was in college I programmed computers to play chess, I wrote papers that were published in international conferences on artificial intelligence, I got As in every practical programming-related class (other than Fortran, ugh!), and then, by the way, I got a full scholarship to go to graduate school for two years.

Then, when I finally had a job in the "real world" at HBO, the television network, my programming was so bad (awful!) I had to go to courses offered at AT&T for two months in order to get my programming in shape. And even then I was still nowhere near ready to do real programming in the real world. It probably took about another six months of daily effort to learn how to really program. I had the passion for computers and I'm sure if all I had done were those AT&T courses right from the beginning I would've been fine.

*

By the way, it was my passion more than my pedigree that got me a job in the real world. I felt like I was in a fairy tale land when I went to the interview at HBO. These were real people working on real projects and the girls looked a lot different than the types of girls you see on an academic campus. I was READY for this job after spending my entire life among academics.

I was interviewed by four different people. Each one the boss of the other. I knew none of the questions they asked. *"Do you know how to program on a Mac?"* No. *"Do you know UNIX?"* A little but not good enough to program. *"Do you know anything about interactive TV."* Nothing. *"Do you know C++?"* No. *"Do you know anything about object-oriented programming?"* Zero. *"What about GUIs?"* Nothing.

In the hallway I saw an office for someone named "Winnie Ho". I had to work at a place with someone with that name.

But no such luck. I didn't know anything despite majoring in computer science and going to graduate school for computer science.

I left the building. Called my girlfriend, *"looks like I won't be moving to NYC after all."* She was relieved but I wasn't. I had no other way of breaking up with her.

Right outside of the HBO building was Bryant Park. Chess tables were set up. Asa Hoffman was at one of the tables playing. I happened to know who he was because my dad, 30 years earlier, had dropped out of grad school when he was playing too much chess with Asa. I sat down to play him. He didn't remember my dad at all. Whatever. We started playing. I won!

I looked up and there was the boss of the boss of the guy who would be my boss if I got a job at HBO. He was watching the whole game! We took a walk around the park. He was a ranked chess player also. *"I can't believe you beat Asa,"* he said. *"I never saw anyone do that."*

We talked for about an hour about everything but computers. A week later he called me and said I had the job. He asked me how much I made at my current job. I lied and said a number 50% higher than what I was making. He said, *"ok, we can offer you that."*

*

Sometimes you have to throw a kid in the water to teach them how to swim (or let them fail so they can learn. Not "drown" since we're not animals). That's the way to learn. Not being force-fed from textbooks written twenty years ago and being taught by professors with little real world experience. It's a shame also that unless you have a PhD, a college won't let you teach (in most cases). PhDs are often the most intellectual but have the least real world experience. And for that great experience we have to go into massive debt now.

Q: Do you have any advice for students who are in college right now and feel like they aren't getting anything out of their education?

Yes, take a year or two off and try some of my eight alternatives.

Q: Are there many people who disagree with your thoughts? Agree? How do people react when they first hear what you have to say?

I think many people agree and don't say anything. But the people who disagree get very, very upset, as I discussed earlier. I've even had death threats based on this opinion (see below chapter). People have a huge life attachment to the fact that college is a part of life, the same way that birth, marriage, parenting, and death are. It's not. It's a relatively modern invention (for the mainstream American, it's about fifty years old; the idea that most kids should go to college, after 6000 years of civilization). Unfortunately this modern invention has been so abused by college administrators that the next generation of kids we graduate will be mired down in debt, and STILL need to learn the skills required for basic jobs that they want to do. Let's not forget, nobody learns how to be a doctor in college. That's pre-med. They learn a little in one or two years of medical school, but then they really learn when they are a resident in an actual hospital. And then between debt, insurance, and the burdens government is now placing on doctors, how will they ever pay down their burdens? The entire system needs to change but the discussion has to happen somewhere. Hopefully it will be here.

Q: ANYTHING ELSE YOU'D LIKE TO ADD?

I began my career at the age of 23, after I left graduate school. And then I began a career from scratch again when I was 26, and then 28, and a totally new career when I was 33, and then a completely new career when I was 36. And now I'm 43 and I'm still open to changing careers and doing new things in life. There's no rush to start a career at the age of 22. Life changes as you go out in the world and experience things. Failures happen; seeds grow and take years to turn into a tree. Give yourself time to plant those seeds, to learn from your failures, to experience new things in life. The earlier you start to do this, the wiser, healthier, and more balanced you will be. You will be more capable of making decisions on career, family, and life in general.

It's also important that people stop using the statistic: people who went to college make more money. This is a very true statistic but anyone who takes Statistics 101 in college should know that correlation is not cause-and-effect. It could quite possibly be that over the past 30 years, people who are more achievement oriented (and hence more likely to make more money) were more likely to go to college. A better test would be if we take 2000 people who got accepted to Harvard today and divide them randomly into 2 groups: one that goes to college, the other that doesn't, and see what they are earning 5, 10, 20, 30 years from now. (Some people will then say, *"but money isn't everything"* and I strongly agree, but this is just to counterbalance that one statistic that seems to suggest money is everything)

DON'T DISCOUNT THE VALUE OF SPENDING TIME EXPERIENCING THE WORLD BEFORE YOU MAKE THE ENORMOUS FINANCIAL COMMITMENT OF GOING TO COLLEGE. It will teach you the beginnings (and JUST the beginnings) of what might be important to you. It will teach you how to survive, it will teach you about people other than from your own age group and socio-economic demographic, it will teach you about the 99% of opportunities that happen in the world that have nothing to do with college, it will teach you how to stretch your mind to learn how to sell and communicate, and finally it will show you at an early age that failure, choices, and life is a spectrum and not a ladder. Take advantage of that when still young and I guarantee you all of life will bend down and support your endeavors.

Why Does Taylor Northcutt Want to Kill me?

After one of my anti-college screeds I got the below email from someone named "Taylor Northcutt."

"I hop that your foolesh feels relizes that peapl in indea are dieing in indea just to go to collige and you have the odasity to tell the world it's a horribil thing. Ill bet that both your douters well think your a complet ass hole when they get older. You making the Us look like a ovly confedent jackass of a country. Pray that i dont find you becase i well kill you with no mercecy then devour your body. I shal never messege you agean Nor shal i reply... we speak no more."

And you know, the first thing I wonder is, how is Taylor Northcutt (whoever he is) going to meet a girl? Like, is he the sort of guy who can mingle at a bar? Does he have the basic social skills?

Because if he doesn't meet someone, and have kids, and then have grandkids, who is going to take care of him when he's an old man? Where's he going to be?

One time my grandma called me and said, *"He's missing?"*

I said, *"Who's missing?"*

"Him. He's missing."

And I said, *"Is grandpa there?"*

And she said, *"They kidnapped him."*

So I went over there and, in fact, my grandpa was missing. According to the neighbor he wasn't feeling well so left to go to the hospital. But my grandma had forgotten that. So I went to the hospital and picked my grandpa up to take him home. As we were walking out of the hospital, shit was coming out of his pants onto the floor. *"I'm sorry,"* he said. IT'S HARD TO BE OLD. I DON'T WANT IT.

So who will take care of Taylor Northcutt when he's old? He needs a woman who can calm him down. Maybe make him go to work instead of sending me emails via Facebook (unless, maybe he's a Facebook employee, or perhaps even Mark Zuckerberg, just having some fun) I tried to click on his profile but it was already gone or deleted or something. It wasn't clickable and I had never seen that before on Facebook. I reported it on Facebook (if Facebook can't help him meet a woman then I don't know who can) but no response yet.

We just want to be happy. Every day I find myself angry about lots of different things. I GET ANGRY at people I think have done me wrong. I GET ANGRY at people who tell me one thing but then it turns out they were lying. I GET ANGRY at people who are overly defensive about things I say. Or people who take articles I've written and turn them around into something I haven't written just so they have an excuse to be angry at me. I GET ANGRY thinking about my neighbor who was angry at me for some reason that (I thought) didn't make sense. I GET ANGRY at people who don't call me back. I GET ANGRY at people who aren't doing things I think they should be doing.

It's so hard to live one goddamn day without feeling any anger. And yet ANGER IS LINKED TO CANCER, HEART DISEASE, STROKES (my dad had a fatal stroke while in an argument with a real estate agent), etc.

We know for a fact that if we feel less anger we'll be happier, we'll live longer, our days will be more productive, we might even laugh more, which leads to further health benefits.

But we've all been through a lot. It's been a hard ten years. People don't admit it but we've all had our moments in the past ten years where we felt like we were going to break loose at the seams. The threads holding us together twisting out of control until we are just strings floating in the air. So we find things to be angry about, to lash out, because it seems that's the only way to hold the threads together. The only way we can preserve the sense of self that has slowly been lost over the past few years.

One of my daughters gets angry quite a bit these days. I don't know what to do with her. I tell her to take deep breaths and count to ten. But it's hard for a little girl. I love her so much and want to hold her when she's angry and I try not to tell her about her future. Because her future is me and it might not be so pleasant.

So here are my techniques for avoiding anger when I can:

REMEMBER IT'S UNIVERSAL. Realize that everyone is in pain. Every-one had a bad day this morning. They looked in the mirror and they weren't happy about what they saw. Or they are having prob-lems with a girl. Or their parents or kids or wife are disappointed in them. Or their father didn't love them when they were kids. So now they are taking it out on me. Just staying aware of that helps to reduce my judgments of them.

BODY: Different types of anger affect me in different parts of my body. If I'm angry at myself, for instance, I feel it in my stomach. If I'm angry at someone I work with, I feel it in my head, almost like a headache. If I'm angry at someone in my family, I feel it more in my chest. Just realizing where in the body the anger is affecting me, and recognizing when I'm feeling it, helps me to stop the anger in its tracks.

JUDGMENT: Anger, when it comes from judgment, is a form of ego. I think I'm not so good at judging people. Usually I dislike people the first time I meet them. And I think all sorts of things about them that are not true. Again, just recognizing this is happening helps me to avoid doing it.

PARANOIA: A lot of my anger comes from paranoia. Is he doing a deal without me? Is she cheating on me? Some of this seems to be genetic – my late Alzheimer's grandma assuming someone kidnapped my grandpa. She could never say "hello" when she picked up the phone. She always had to grunt until someone talked so she knew it wasn't anyone who was "after" her. When I get this paranoid feeling all I can do is pray. Please God, help me stop being paranoid. And I just have to wait until the feeling goes away. Or take a pill. Either one.

GOSSIP: I try never to gossip about anyone. If I never say anything bad behind someone's back then I can at least feel comfortable that nobody has any reason to do the same with me.

BREATHE: I try to breathe deeply as much as I can throughout the day. When I'm angry I take short, shallow breaths. The air is barely in my throat before I'm exhaling it again. So in anticipation of later anger, I try to do the opposite. Take deep breaths as often as possible. I try to get air going into every part of my body. I read something beautiful the other day – that when you breathe in, imagine that you are inviting God in. When you breathe out, imagine that you are surrendering yourself to God. If I surrender enough, then I know I won't get angry.

IT'S HOPELESS. A few months ago, someone wanted to allocate $25mm for me to manage. A friend of mine ended up blocking the deal and making it not happen. I was angry at him. I even sent an angry note. He wrote back, *"What's wrong James? We're friends. It was just business."*

Nothing is ever just business. It's all about relationships and trust. But in business, people lie to you and misrepresent every day. I can count up to 100 the number of times I've been lied to in just the past three or four months by people I consider or considered friends. People think nothing of it in business and then they just move on. And no matter how "Zen" I get about it, I can't lie to myself – I'm going to be angry. And I'm going to think at night about it. And compose emails in my heads. And talk to my friends about it. And so on.

So the best thing to do is to get away from it. Every day, eliminate people who get you angry, and surround yourself (if you can) with people who don't.

At the end of the day we want to be able to handle our suffering and increase our happiness. Those are really the only goals. To do that, the most important thing is health. To keep health, we need to reduce anger. It's really simple.

When I was six years old, my grandfather would tell me, *"You know why the universe goes on forever?"*

"Why?" I always responded.

"Because if it ever ended," he said, *"then what's on the other side?"*

But it was so hard to think about. What does forever mean?

"Think about it," he said. *"What's on the other side?"*

So when I got that email from Taylor Northcutt, all I could think was that same question: *"What's on the other side?"*

Owning a Home

I'm not saying you should never own a home again. Do whatever you want. But I want to figure out why for 40 years people have told me that they NEED to own a home to feel happy, to feel like they have "roots," so that their kids can be happier, etc. Using "the kids" here is a convenient excuse. Kids don't care. Kids want to be loved. They don't need an in-ground swimming pool, they need attention, love, nutrition, laughter, play.

The "roots" idea is an interesting dynamic. That somehow a home that is 80% owned by the bank anyway gives you some visceral connection to the planet, to Mother Earth, to the bounty of natural resources the planet uses to restore itself, to feed and sustain us. Owning a home, versus renting, somehow feels like it connects us to those roots.

It's not true. It's programming by the machine. By the banks, the corporations, the government, that wants you in hock, inflexible, and eventually in trouble. So they need your help. Again.

I've lost a home when I went broke. I describe it in my first book. I describe it on my blog. But that's not what has created my opinions on home ownership (although it certainly confirmed them). It was a horrible feeling each month. Not everyone experiences what I went through although in the past decade many have felt it. I had no job. Every month cash was running out at the bank, expenses were going up, the house was standing still and nobody wanted to buy it, and eventually I would be unable to buy diapers and food for my children.

This wasn't just me. In the last decade this has happened to a lot of people. I would go to my bank and say, *"interest rates are now lower: How about I refinance at the lower interest so I can pay a lower interest rate?"* And they would say, *"No, your house is now appraised lower."* But, I would say, you are the guys who appraised my house in the first place at the high interest rate. Doesn't it make sense now that a lower interest rate would make it easier for you to get your loan back.

But common sense has an unusual attraction to deaf ears.

So the clock would tick. And I would get closer to losing my "roots." Being torn from Mother Earth, thrust out into the endless vacuum of space. At least that's the metaphysical fear rooted deep down.

And where do we get that fear? The trillion dollar banking industry absolutely depends on us perpetuating the myth generation after generation that roots are a good thing. That paying interest to them is a good thing. That potentially defaulting and risking foreclosure is a sacrifice we need to take. That being inflexible about where we live and what jobs we can go for is also part of that sacrifice. That kids need a stable lifestyle, and so on.

And maybe they are right. Again, this book isn't about judging. And this part of the book isn't meant to be ranting (although I seem to be doing a good job of being on the borderline of a constant rant).

But let's look again at the opposite. What if one doesn't own a home? You have more cash in the bank (no down payment), less debt, more flexibility for jobs (because you can live anywhere), more flexibility if you lose a job or come under some financial stress, more opportunities to travel and live in different locales.

Are these things horrible? They might be. Its part of the reason why when I did a video on this topic for AOL it got over 2mm views and thousands of comments arguing each side. Ditto for when I did it for a video at Yahoo.com as well.

And then a guy even wrote a rebuttal to my argument. I respond below:

Why I Would Rather Shoot Myself In the Head Than Own a Home

I only had one friend in MySpace when I joined in 2005. "Tom." In fact, all 100 million people who had joined MySpace had one friend. "Tom." He welcomed us all to our new cyber home and made us feel as comfortable as possible there. "Tom" is Tom Anderson, a cofounder of the MySpace, the first member of the 100 million people community and automatic friend to everyone who signed up.

So, through a strange set of circumstances and coincidences, that very same Tom just emailed me. A great crime had been committed against me. Tom Anderson, my first friend on MySpace, wanted me to know about it.

Somebody had disagreed with me.

Tom sent me a link to a site, "realtytrac.com"

He wrote me, *"Btw, saw a rebuttal to your home-ownership article today that I thought you might be interested in:"*

Someone named Rick Sharga wrote a column there arguing against my recent column: *Why I would Never own a Home Again.*

IT TOOK RICK ONLY ABOUT FOUR LINES TO INSULT ME which shows he doesn't read my stuff very closely. He said I would probably recommend that people buy "stocks" or my "fund of funds." IN OTHER WORDS, HE'S SUGGESTING THAT THE ONLY REASON I COULD HAVE AN OPINION IS OUT OF COMPLETE SELF-INTEREST. I guess in most cases that's how the world works, which is a shame. I have no self-interest at all in this opinion. I want to help people.

My theory is that complete honesty frees me from the shackles that bind me to stress, anxiety, financial insecurity, spiritual insecurity, and so on. Most people who read my blog think that I'm almost sabotaging my self interest by revealing all that I do. In fact, it's the reverse. My self-interest is freedom in my head.

For instance, in contrast to Mr. Sharga's opinions on my self-interest, see the Chapter on "10 Reasons You Should Never Own Stocks Again". And, I also happen to think most hedge funds are scams and would never run a fund of hedge funds again. So, all self-interest is out.

I legitimately believe that people would be happier if they don't mortgage their lives away, if they don't fall into the myth of the

WAS BLIND BUT NOW I SEE

white picket fence leading to happiness. If they pull themselves away from the American Religion and find their own path to follow.

So Mr. Sharga starts off already being completely wrong by misrepresenting me to his readers. But that's fine. People seem to do that all the time.

Next he makes his argument with another highly intelligent point:

"The context that Mr. Altucher lays out is actually more hysterical than historical. The notion that homeownership was some sort of deep, dark conspiracy foisted on innocent rubes by diabolical business owners to keep them permanently grounded (and therefore, unable to escape their low wage, dead end jobs) is just pointy-headed nonsense."

I do not have a pointy head. It's more block-headed. But, it's a fact that many early factories would often provide housing for their employees and then charge them for the "rent" and deduct it from their salaries. This was a standard technique only 100 years ago. Often employees would get in debt to the factories, keeping them, in fact, "grounded."

Let's get even more hysterical. Let's look at the trillion dollar banking industry. This is the best business in the world, until it isn't (2008).

How do banks make money? Very simple. They borrow from you at cheap interest rates and then lend to you at higher interest rates. What? How do they do that? Well, when they pay you 0.5% on your checking account, it's as if they are borrowing from you at a very cheap interest rate. When they then turn around and give you a 6% mortgage loan, they are lending to you. They make money on the difference between the 6% and the 0.5%. It's a great business and I often advise people to become the bank when they have that opportunity.

It's such a great business, in fact, that banks have spent 200 years drilling it into us with billions in advertising that the "American Dream" is to own the white picket fence, the paved driveway, maybe borrow more to make an extension to the house. Put in a swimming pool. Tear down some walls. Nobody can ever kick you out.

56

You're not flushing your rent down the toilet. You're owning! You're keeping up with the Joneses (the most successful, yet mysterious, family in American mythology, that we all have to keep up with. What happens behind closed doors when the beatings occur, when little Bobby Jones cries himself to sleep, the Joneses will never tell us) At least, in 30 years you will own. But at least you've fixed in a mortgage rate so inflation won't kill you. And having your own home means you now have "roots."

As Mr. Sharga says: *"Simply going back to the beginnings of the U.S., the concepts of 'wealth' and 'land ownership' went hand-in-hand."* I guess that's true. I can't find it in the Constitution anywhere but the man knows what he's talking about.

He also states: *"going back to medieval times, the feudal lords basically were land barons; the serfs, the working poor of the age, were allowed to live on the lands in exchange for paying exorbitant amounts of money to the lords. However, much the lords decided to collect. Or you could leave (on your own, or in pieces). Sounds like a renter's lot in life to me."*

I'M A SERF AND ALWAYS WILL BE. I'll never be a "feudal lord." Fortunately, because of innovation, entrepreneurship, and the rise of economic growth throughout most of the world, the life of a "serf" right now is probably one million times better than any feudal lord could've ever hoped for back then. Here are some benefits of being a serf right now:

MORE CASH. You never have to put down a down payment that uses up most of the cash in your bank account. You're never going to see that cash again if you use it as a downpayment. It's just gone into an illiquid investment and when you most need it, that's when you are most likely not able to get at it.

LESS DEBT. It's true a mortgage locks in your payment. But you're greatly in debt so you are paying interest straight to the bank that has nothing to do with increasing your ownership. In many cases it will take 20 to 30 years before you stop paying that extra interest to the bank.

LESS INFLATION RISK. Property taxes often go up faster than inflation whereas usually rent does not go up faster than inflation (by definition, since government calculated inflation uses rents instead of home prices).

No maintenance. Homeowners have to take care of all maintenance. Some years that might be nothing (unlikely) and some years that may go up much faster than inflation.

Less overall costs. When property taxes and maintenance go up faster than inflation it means you are probably not covering the costs (plus the mortgage) via renting.

More flexibility. In a global economy, opportunities can be anywhere. I like having my flexibility.

In other words, if you are a feudal lord today, you are laying out more cash than the renter/serf, and being caught in the spider web of escalating costs in every direction. Whereas the serf has only one payment, which is often contractually laid out for years (I have a contract that specifies my rent for the next five years with my option to renew).

Which means that the serf can diversify his portfolio to a much greater extent than the feudal baron and the serf can more easily move to take advantage of opportunities in other geographical areas (as opposed to the serfs of medieval times that Mr. Sharga compares us to).

That down payment that the feudal baron put out will only go up in value if housing goes up in value and it is completely illiquid and usually a major part of his portfolio (little diversification). And he's flushing money down the toilet with interest (which usually doesn't go up with inflation), property taxes (which often go up faster than inflation), and maintenance (which goes up with inflation).

The serf is flushing money down with rent. But has more cash in the bank, a more diversified portfolio, and is generating liquid cash (hopefully) from other investments. Or has the cash to be an entrepreneur, move around to take advantage of other opportunities, etc. This (in my experience) more than makes up for the rent.

Some people, for their own personal reasons, like to own a home. I have nothing against that. Go for it. Just make sure it's not because of the hypnosis provided by the American banking industry which props up the American Mythology.

MR. SHARGA GIVES A PARTING SHOT AT ME. I'm not sure why. I've never met the man. Nor am I saying anything bad about him here. Just commenting on his article. But he seems to know me pretty well to make generalizations about me and my personality: *"For Mr. Altucher, the notion of homeownership seems downright scary. And he shouldn't own a home. He probably shouldn't own a car either — or a goldfish. He wants the combination of limited responsibility, someone else 'taking care of things,' and the ability to move to Sri Lanka on a moment's notice. And he wants his investments to all be liquid (so maybe I should re-think the goldfish part)."*

He's absolutely right about all of those things. I would never own a goldfish (disgusting) and I lease my car (well, my wife does. You need a license to own a car). And I love the fact that I can move to Sri Lanka at a moment's notice although I actually really like where I live right now. And owning a home is downright scary to me. Leveraging up 400% in an illiquid investment with no diversification is a scary concept to me and should be to any rational person.

I don't like to quote people without their permission. But I'm grateful Tom Anderson pointed out that article to me because I think the article misrepresents some of the things I said by implying I have self-interest attached to my opinion (I have zero). Tom has already experienced great success as an entrepreneur and will continue to do so. As he states in his email to me: *"The fact that I'm finding articles on realtytrac might give you some idea of what I'm up to."*

Tom Anderson is going to succeed at whatever he sets his mind to. As for Mr. Sharga, I'm going to give him constructive criticism. He shouldn't try to bring me down ("self-interest," "scared to own a goldfish," "hysterical," etc.) to make his point. That's bad writing in general. He should read my *"33 Unusual Tips to Being a Better Writer"* in my previous book and the next time he lays out his argument I'm sure it will be better.

[Incidentally, you can get my previous book for free if you email luckiestpersonalive@gmail.com with the subject line "How to be the luckiest person alive"]

Will housing be a great investment? Who knows? There will be many great investments out there in the years to come. Innovation is not ending. A year ago nobody owned an iPad. Google is making cars that drive on highways without drivers, companies are curing cancer, and when I finish my teleportation machine things are going to get a lot better around here.

Last night my oldest daughter went to her first middle-school dance. She had a fun time and is sleeping late in her room. This morning, hopefully, the rain will stop because my youngest daughter is begging me to walk her to the river even though it's pouring. I had an orange for breakfast and I still might convince Claudia to make me waffles. This morning, in my self-interest, everyone is happy in my house

The US Constitution Has Been Mangled

I get a lot of emails. Many positive and friendly. But many have points to prove. Things they need to get off their chest and I'm the one somehow they need to prove their point to. I have never in one way or the other ever acknowledged a political affiliation. I'm disgusted with all politics.

But this person wrote me an email detailing the growth of the US (in GDP terms) under all Democrat Presidents and Republican Presidents since 1948 and concluded, "SEE! THE DEMOCRATS ARE BETTER!"

I won't get into the numbers but there was approximately a 0.2% difference overall. In other words, no real difference. And I guess that 0.2% difference can be largely attributed to the growth of the

Internet in the 90s under Clinton. Did Clinton create that boom? Probably not.

For me, all the Presidents are bad. History will tell with "O." But with "W" we are in two wars and have spent over 3 trillion dollars killing people there in retaliation for 9/11 when we could've been avoiding a financial crisis. With Clinton, he was, to be frank, getting blowjobs and defending against impeachment when he could've been on the case with Al Quaeda, and on and on. I can go back through every President since George Washington who I think was the only decent President we ever had.

In fact, below I describe my reasons for completely abolishing the institution of the Presidency.

But the important point is this: why was this guy so proud to be a "Democrat" and so eager to label me something else. We label ourselves because we want to be part of something we perceive as better than us as an individual. We can't handle our individuality, the strength of ourselves as a single human.

Labeling also gives us a convenient excuse for the anger and the fear that is begging to escape our small minds. If I'm X, then I can be angry at people who are the opposite of X. Or even better, I can be afraid of them AND THEN angry at them.

I don't like to label myself anything. I'm the dumbest guy in the room and happy to stay that way. Then everyone else can fight. I can listen and learn.

Politics is a Scam – Why I Will Never Vote Again

I had five seconds to make the secretive most powerful man in the world like me so I could potentially make millions. *"James,"* Bill McCluskey said to me, *"this is Alan Quasha."* Bill was CEO of Brean Murray, one of the mini-banks I considered selling my fund of hedge funds to in 2006. We had a deal on the table and I was desperate at the time to make it work. The table was circular, there were papers on it with numbers, I was bullshitting every which way I could about "synergies." Whatever. That was months later. But first I had to meet Alan Quasha, the owner of Brean Murray, at an event they were throwing, AND HE HAD TO LIKE ME. Because...

(Have you heard of Alan Quasha before this post? And there he is with Ivan Boesky's daughter. Go figure.)

Alan Quasha squinted his eyes, shook my hand. He had no idea who I was. I certainly wasn't anything like George W. Bush, the man Quasha had personally saved in 1986. In 1986, Bush was CEO of some oil company that was going down in flames. Possibly the worst oil company in Texas history.

Some calls were made and Quasha's Harken Oil bought Bush's company for millions of dollars. Then, of course, a few years later, Bush sold his shares in Quasha's Harkin Oil right before Harkin Oil announced a mega-loss and the stock tanked. Bush used his profit's to buy a stake in the Texas Rangers, sold that stake later for 10-15 million dollars and was finally able to follow his father's sage advice ("don't go into politics until you get rich" ***).

LET'S SPELL OUT WHAT THAT MEANS: if Alan Quasha called up W on September 12, 2001 in the middle of Bush pouring over maps of the jungles of Afghanistan to see where we would invade (do they have jungles in Afghanistan? Do we really need an "h" in Afghanistan?), Bush would say *"hold all calls,"* close the doors of the Oval Office and say *"Hi Daddy Number 2,"* to Quasha. He owed his life, his livelihood, the Texas Rangers, the Presidency, all to Alan Quasha and now I was shaking Quasha's hand. I had five seconds to make Alan Quasha like me almost as much as he liked Bush so he would buy my company. Why? Alan Quasha was Chairman of Brean Murray.

Fast-forward about ten seconds. Alan Quasha had moved on. Now I was being introduced to Terry Mcauliffe. Terry was the Vice-Chairman of Brean Murray. Terry was known in most circles as "BILL CLINTON'S BEST FRIEND." Terry raised the bulk of the money for the two Presidential campaigns that Bill was in (the first, of course, where he crushed Bush, the Elder). I'm guessing Terry also raised the money for all of Hillary's political races. If Chelsea Clinton ever ran for Mayor of New York (now that Weiner is out of the running so you never know) I bet Terry would raise all the money for her race as well.

SO THERE YOU HAVE IT. The biggest mastermind in REPUBLICAN politics, the behind the scenes mover and shaker across the entire Bush family, was Chairman of the company. And the biggest mover-and-shaker in DEMOCRAT politics, was Vice Chairman. The war of values, between Democracy and Republicanism that our founders had fought for, had shed blood for, was over between them, if it ever even existed. Screw "The Federalist Papers!" Let's make some money!

You see why your vote is useless? Not only is it useless, it's scary. A female friend of mine told me: *"it was like the biggest orgasm I had felt in the past 10 years of my marriage"* when Obama became President.

But then what happened? Obama extended Bush's tax cuts, kept Bush's Secretary of Defense, extended the wars in Afghanistan and Iraq, didn't close Guantanamo Bay, and fought for a healthcare that's now being disputed (and overturned) in every court in America. What else has he done? I can't think of it. Planned Parenthood has less government funding now than under Bush. Africa has less funding from the US than under Bush (in fact, Obama has bombed Africa / Libya).

And yet we all fought so much. *"Palin is an idiot!"* *"Biden can't speak straight!"* *"Where's Obama's birth certificate!"* *"Is McCain senile?"* *"!""!""!"*"!" Let's fight in the streets and pass out pamphlets and wear buttons and lose friends *("I can't believe he's voting for Nader!")* and stick on bumper stickers that can never be scratched off once we realize they are as embarrassing as that magic dragon tattoo we got lasered across our backs when we were 17.

We fought so hard for beliefs we all thought we had and where do they all end up? Where does it all congeal together right before it flushes down the toilet?

Answer: One is Chairman and the other is Vice-Chairman of the same company. They're all laughing together. Slapping backs. Making Money. They are laughing at you and me, my friend. The war is over for them.

We voted them all in there, they served their time, and now they are minting money as if they own the printing press. I watched Quasha and McCaulliffe laugh, sitting next to each other when they used to pretend to be sitting so far apart.

They have no idea who I am, what I want out of life, what ideas I think are good or bad, or would save the world, or whatever. They were laughing as hard as they could just ten feet from me and I knew while I stood there watching them, hoping beyond hope that they would share some of the wealth, I knew that they were laughing at me.

*** *Net worth of most recent Presidents* and Vice-Presidents (according to celebritynetworth.com)

- Barack Obama: $5 million (will probably end up around a billion)

- George W. Bush: $26 million

- Bill Clinton $85 million (my guess is this is understated by about $50-100 million.)

- George H.W Bush: $15 million (I think this is understated by about a billion)

- And now the big question: Al Gore versus Dick Cheney? Democrats versus Republicans. The winner is...

- Al Gore, coming in at $300 million with Dick Cheney at $90 million (don't forget Gore was an advisor to Google since 2001 and on the Board of Apple. He also manages a billion dollar "green fund"). Al Gore's net worth in 2001: $1 million.

My Visit With The President of The United States

(Or...My First Experience With Politics)

On my 12th birthday in 1980 I called early in the morning to con-firm my appointment at the White House. Specifically, I had a meeting scheduled with Rex Scouten, the Chief Usher of the White House. In other words, Jimmy Carter's butler. I had spoken to him several weeks earlier when I "interviewed" him for a local newspa-per. I had casually mentioned to him that I was planning on going to Washington DC for my 12th birthday and could I stop by and see him to interview him in person. Of course, he said, I would be happy to personally give you a tour of the White House. A little off the beaten track, he said.

Being 12 years old, I had no plans to be in Washington DC on any day at all, particularly my birthday which was falling on a school day. In fact, I had zero control over my life and wasn't even allowed to be on the phone that afternoon, talking to the Chief Usher of the White House and a man that served every President from Harry Truman until his eventual retirement during the Clinton years.

The prior month's phone bill had been over $700 for all my calls to the "202" area code (from what seemed to me to be a very close "201" but somehow or other you would think I was bankrupting my parents the way they acted every time a phone bill came in. The last time they were so upset my dad yelled at me: *"Your entire inheri-tance from your grandfather is going to pay the November phone bill!"*)

But I used a technique that's worked for me many times since then – I *"faked it till I made it."* As far as Rex Scouten was concerned, I was coming to Washington DC on my birthday. Later that eve-ning I said to my dad: *"Dad , I have an appointment with the Presi-dent of the United States on my birthday."*

I showed him a letter Rex Scouten had sent me after I had first interviewed him, stating that I can stop by any time. So my dad arranged for himself to have some business over in Washington (I

65

had no concept what he did for a living but if possible, please, could we stay at the Watergate Hotel?) and we were off to DC.

I had to keep busy while I was there. I wasn't meeting "Rex" until the afternoon so I needed to fill up my morning or else it would be a waste. So I called my local congressman and he agreed to meet. And his incoherent senile blathering almost made me late for my other important meetings. I met with Senator Dale Bumpers from Arkansas, who I interviewed (I asked him if he wanted to be the Vice-Presidential candidate and he said he enjoyed being a Senator too much), Senator Nancy Kassenbaum from Kansas (I was in love with her), I ran into Tip O'Neill, the Speaker of the House, in the hallway but he was surrounded by people so I couldn't talk to him.

I showed up unannounced at Senator Birch Bayh's office (father of Evan Bayh). And guess what? It was his birthday also! So his staff brought in his birthday cake and sang Happy Birthday to both of us. My dad joined up with me and we met with Sen. Paul Tsongas from Massachusetts. He said he hoped Ted Kennedy would win the primaries so he could be the senior senator from Massachusetts instead of the junior senator from Massachusetts. He later quit the Senate when he found out he had terminal cancer saying, *"I never met a man on his deathbed who said he wished he had spent more time at work."*

Later, we went to the White House, and while we were waiting for Scouten, we saw Carter, Mondale, and other random people walking down a hallway. Scouten came in then and gave us a private tour of the White House. Later that night I called Lori Gumbinger, who, along with Senator Nancy Kassenbaum, was the current love of my life, and told her I saw the President but *"didn't get a chance to speak with him."*

For the next few months I made non-stop phone calls to everyone I could. I was a phone addict. I'd get home from school and start dialing "202" all over the place. Both my parents worked and once General Hospital, the soap opera, was over (I had to see if Luke and Laura were going to stop Mikhos Cassadine from taking over the world) I got to work. "202," "202," "202."

I interviewed for the local newspaper every Senator who would return my call. Sometimes in the morning I'd wait outside, crouched behind a bush in the backyard, until I heard the garage door open and close twice, signaling that both my parents were gone for the day, then I'd go back in and get an early start on the phone calls.

Not only would I run up my parent's bill but I'd run up my unemployed older sister's bill, charging phone calls to her "212" number. How else was I going to talk to Bill Bradley? Or Jim Boren, who was specifically running to be Ted Kennedy's Vice-Presidential candidate with the campaign motto "When in doubt, mumble". Or the time I had to hide in the locked laundry room, interviewing billionaire (and Libertarian Party VP Candidate) David Koch while my grandmother banged on the door, *"who are you talking to in there!"*

Finally, I can't remember his name, but I got a phone call from the editor-in-chief of "The Home News," the local newspaper serving central New Jersey. *"Is this James Altucher?"* he asked.

"Yes."

"Listen," he said, *"we just got a call from the Senator Paul Sarbanes' office asking about you. You can't keep calling Senators saying you are writing for The Home News. You're 12 years old. I have guys who went to graduate school in Journalism who I can't even hire right now. I'm certainly not going to let you have a column in this newspaper."*

I went home thinking my career as a writer was over before it even began. We all have dreams as a child. And we all have childish dreams. Even at the age of 43 I still have childish dreams. And in many ways, I still consider myself a child. But every dream I have, I KNOW will come true. Whether they do or not.

Abolish The Presidency – It's a Useless Job Anyway

WE'RE ALL GEARING UP NOW for the biggest extravaganza since Bristol Palin was on *Dancing With the Stars*. The Presidential Election of 2012. Everyone is so excited! Will Obama come back from his dismal low ratings and break the record (nobody has ever come back from such a low rating in their first administration to win). Will Mitt Romney or Jon Huntsman settle their Mormon differences? Will Rick Perry win or secede from the Union? Will Michelle Bachmann release a sex video?

We have no idea. But we know something will happen. And lots of it. It's going to cost $2 billion to win this election according to the latest pundit analysis ("pundit" "anal" and "sis" being the key words here). There's going to be a lot of smoking behind closed doors. A lot of deal-making. A lot of machines are going to kick into gear. Consultants will become rich. TV networks and newspapers will get down on their knees and praise god they get to survive another year thanks to the massive amounts of advertising.

HERE'S MY QUESTION: WHAT DOES THE PRESIDENT EVEN DO? DO WE NEED ONE?

In fact, one step further: I think the institution of the Presidency has largely ruined my life and the lives of most other people.

MY PROPOSAL: WE DON'T NEED A PRESIDENT OF THE UNITED STATES. IN FACT, HE'S USELESS.

First off, the Constitution doesn't even address the powers of the Presidency until Article II. The Founders clearly thought the legislative branch was more important, i.e. the actual branch that creates laws, declares wars, etc.

But, in a article on my blog I've already written that THERE'S NO LONGER A NEED FOR A LEGISLATIVE BRANCH the way the Founders conceived it. Times have changed and technology has driven away all of the initial reasons for a republic-based legislative branch so we can have a true democracy commanded by a much more informed electorate:

JUST TO SUMMARIZE MY PRIOR ARTICLE: The only original reasons the founding fathers had for an elected legislative branch (a republic instead of a democracy) were:

There was no way to transmit information quickly to the voters (now we have the internet so everyone can actually vote and be informed).

The founding fathers figured only rich landowners could afford to be congressmen (still mostly true) so that their interests above all would be represented (again, not a true democracy but more a bastardized distortion of one).

So now, we could:

- Save the $4bb in costs that is the budget of congress each year.
- Save the trillion or so in costs that are all the *"you vote for my bridge and I'll vote for yours"* pork that happens.
- Save the 10s of billions in lobbying costs each year (not it would cost 100s of billions to do the same lobbying via advertising instead of just taking a congressman out for dinner).
- Avoid all the fear-mongering and partisanship that was caused by the debt ceiling argument and other similar meaningless arguments.
- Actually have mothers vote on whether or not to send their kids to war.

Ok, enough on that.

SO WHAT'S THE PRESIDENCY FOR? According to the Constitution:

WARS? Lately the President has been declaring wars. We're in Iraq, Afghanistan, Libya, and probably three or four other places I don't even know about. The only problem is, according to the Constitution, THE PRESIDENT IS NOT ALLOWED TO DECLARE WARS. Only the House is. The last war the House has actually declared (the only body of government actually allowed to declare war) was World War II, in 1941. And that was after 11 million people were already killed or about to be killed. Oops! Too late!

So the President, I guess, took "actions" in Korea, Vietnam, Iraq, Afghanistan, Grenada (??), and a dozen other places I would never want to step foot in. [See also: *"Name me one war that was justified"* on my blog]

It's such a simple math: if you get rid of the Presidency, millions of American children will live to be adults instead of dying on foreign soil. And millions of civilians in other countries would be left alone. Seems like a good deal.

TREATIES. Since 2000 there's only been two important treaties that have been ratified, both dealing with the US and Russia limiting nuclear arms. This is clearly important. We don't want people sending around nuclear missiles at each other, which is what I guess would've happened if the President of the United States didn't figure this all out for us. Since this is an important issue (and looks like the ONLY important issue from an international perspective), my guess is we can just elect some specialist in nuclear proliferation to become the "head of nuclear treaties." Then we, the new legislative branch democracy, would vote on whether or not to ratify the treaty. All good.

Guess what? The President doesn't really have any other power. Well, you might say, he is:

COMMANDER IN CHIEF OF THE MILITARY. A couple of points: He's not really commander in chief. I'm not going to make fun of the last few Presidents. But if you do the slightest bit of googling on Clinton, Bush, and Obama, you can see that none of them are qualified to be Commander in Chief of a Girl Scout unit, let alone the Army, the Air Force, the Navy, etc.

Second, since the House hasn't declared war since 1941, what's the big deal about being Commander in Chief of an Army that hasn't legally done anything since 1941. I know, I know, we've been in a lot of wars, justified or not. They are "defending my way of life," etc. etc.

Here's what's really defending my way of life. Not somebody fighting in a jungle in Vietnam or Afghanistan but global capitalism. The more we trade and do business and support the economic development of third world countries, the less likely they are to want to bomb us (which has happened once in 50 years and not by a country but by a terrorist group that we successfully fought more through seizing bank accounts than through military actions).

Let's not forget: WE CREATED AL QUAEDA TO fight the Russians. And then we abandoned them: militarily and economically. Let's stop doing that! Bad America!

My solution: eliminate 90% of the ground forces. Keep enough of the Air Force around so we can retaliate if anyone really does invade us. And keep the Navy around so we can ensure that Somalian pirates don't get in the way of free trade. "But what if China invades us?" you might say. Well, I have nothing against good Chinese food but think about it: CHINA ALREADY HAS INVADED US. They have $2 trillion of our dollars. We only have $80 billion of our dollars in the US Treasury. As Bush would say, "*Mission Accomplished!*"

LAWS: From the Constitution: *"He shall from time to time give to the Congress Information of the State of the Union, and recommend to their Consideration such Measures as he shall judge necessary and expedient;"*

I totally forgot about that. He can RECOMMEND things to us. He can have OPINIONS. THAT'S AMAZING!

How can I forget that? Like he can recommend the Department of Education which, since it's creation, the US has gone from #1 in the world in education to #18. Or he can recommend that Fannie Mae reduce their lending standards so that more people can afford homes (eventually causing the housing bust, financial crisis, etc). My guess is, we'd all be better off if the President watched back episodes of *Snooki* on *Jersey Shore* all day instead of recommending things.

Instead, let's have a digg or reddit-style system where people recommend things, back it up with essays, facts, etc and have people rank the recommendations. Then the top 100 ideas ranked gets

voted on by... the legislative branch, which is now the direct electorate instead of a bunch of buffoons we elect who don't really represent our interests.

SUPREME COURT. He can recommend judges to the Supreme Court
that the House has to then ratify. Again, I propose a digg-like system where judges present their credentials and the 150mm non-
children in the United States vote them up or down and when we
need a new Supreme Court Justice we decide which, of the top 10
should be that justice. And we do it through voting. Why should
Supreme Court Justices be judges for life? Same system should be
made for Ambassadors.

FINALLY, THE LAST THING, THE PRESIDENT CAN DO. HE CAN THROW
PARTIES! That's right. This is in Article II, Section 3 of the Constitution. When a visiting Ambassador comes and visits us, the President is allowed to throw a party to greet him. There's usually a very
nice dinner. Then a dance. Then maybe a movie or a show. And a
receiving line where lots of people can spread germs kissing each
other and shaking hands. And everyone dresses in tuxedos. Why
do we need a President to do it? How about Martha Stewart? Or
that other lady on the Food Channel. Or Wolfgang Puck. I nomi-
nate Wolfgang Puck for party-thrower.

THERE'S' NOTHING ELSE THE PRESIDENT CAN DO LEGALLY. All of
the other stuff is artificial. He can go to funerals. He can create
new cabinet level departments (Education, HUD, etc) that require
massive buildings, budgets, and takes away people from private
industry to give them sinecure BS jobs that last forever. I guess he
runs the CIA so we can spy on people. Like how we spied on people
so we avoided 9/11. Errr...

FAQ:

I need an immediate FAQ here to answer the obvious questions:

WON'T THIS LEAD TO ANARCHY OR A POTENTIAL MILITARY COUP?

I'm just recommending getting rid of one man (and the entire mega
bureaucracy that supports him.) The US runs just fine whenever
the President doesn't get in the way. We could've avoided the hous-

ing crisis, the wars, the massive inflationary budgets and debts, etc. We have governors and local police forces to deal with anarchy. And since I'm also suggesting massive de-militarization (since we haven't had a legal war since 1941) that avoids the chances of any military coup.

WHO WILL VETO STUFF? ISN'T THE PRESIDENT THERE TO CHECK CONGRESS?

Obama has vetoed 2 laws during his administration. W vetoed an entire 11 laws in 8 years, 6 of which were overridden and/or passed with minor changes. So that's an easy one: either let the Supreme Court override stuff (which they do anyway if they deem a law "unconstitutional") or let the people override.

WHAT ELSE DOES THE PRESIDENT DO? DOESN'T HE DO ANYTHING?

No, constitutionally he does nothing more. In all of the Amendments to the Constitution that came later, the only important one dealing with the President and his powers is Amendement 22 which LIMITS the power of the Presidency by saying a President can serve no more than two terms. They did this because Roosevelt, on many occasions, tried to take too much power away from the people, the states, and the Constitution, during his three and a half terms. So, Congress and the States, correctly, limited the powers of the Presidency so that a single man can only run havoc throwing parties for two terms instead of infinite.

IF WE HAD A "TRUE DEMOCRACY" WOULDN'T 51% OF THE PEOPLE VOTE TO PAY THEMSELVES OUT OF THE GOVERNMENT TREASURY?

Duh, that ALREADY happened and nobody stopped it. 51% of the country is on some form of unemployment or other government handouts. Most of those handouts created by Presidential "special actions." Rather than taxing the middle class (the upper classes will always figure out how to avoid taxes. It's hard to touch them) why don't we figure out incentives for the 6 million private businesses to simply hire one more person each. That would completely solve unemployment, would feed millions of people, and create a culture of ambition that would lead to a true trickledown effect. The dollars are already in the system. Every less dollar spent by the public sector will, by definition, be spent in the private sector. Let's get some smart people on this already instead of having the President just write checks to everyone.

WELL, WHAT ABOUT THE VICE-PRESIDENT? DO WE GET RID OF HIM ALSO?

Of course not! Someone needs to go to the funerals of dead Kings of other countries. That's a real boring job. Do you want to stare in the coffins of a lot of dead people and pretend to look somber during the funeral? If someone is willing to do that, then by all means give it to them. In fact, sign me up.

I hereby declare that I am entering the race for VICE PRESIDENT OF THE UNITED STATES.

You Need to Quit Your Job Right Now!

My grandfather had a music store where he sold instruments. He also played banjo in a small "band." But once he started having kids he decided to get a job in the corporate world. To get the safety that corporate America promised him. He got that safety to a large extent. He worked for 40 hard years. He literally got a gold watch when he retired. It was the American dream.

I won't get into the particulars of his job but because of the job he developed cataracts in his eyes (he had to handle heating equipment close to his eyes) and, for all practical purposes, went blind in his old age. After the 40 years of safety, all he could do was sit at home and listen to the radio. One time I had to pick him up at the hospital when he was having problems. He was in his pajamas. Crap was dropping out of them as I walked him out of the hospital and into my car.

"I'm sorry," he said.

"Don't worry about it Grandpa," I said.

Life is hard. Old age is hard. Your job might last for 40 years and then what are you left with to pick up the pieces of the life you left behind. My grandfather loved playing the banjo. That was over for him in 1940. A young man, still in his prime.

And now the myth has gotten even worse. The ocean of safety we thought we had has disappeared. It's time to turn it upside down and reject the people who beg us not to. The tide has come in. We have to understand how the world has changed, and the tools we now have at our disposal to deal with those changes.

The other day I met a guy who had worked for 38 years at GM. He wasn't in the union and he wasn't a high level executive. So consequently, when the rock of corporate safety in America over the past century went bankrupt he got nothing. No pension, no insurance, no savings. The unions got their money. The high level executives got their golden parachutes. The 30,000 in the middle got nothing.

"I thought it was safe," he told me. *"I thought nothing could touch me."*

The American religion wants you to believe that corporate safety is here, that it's going to protect you and your white picket fence and your framed college degree. But it's a lie. The government doesn't care about you. Your bosses don't care about you. And when the desert that rises up to claim you back into it's dust, you'll disappear and nobody will wonder about your accomplishments and the things you are most proud of.

Most people need to begin their exit strategy RIGHT NOW.

Below I give some reasons. But the real key is, everyone needs a bit of freedom in their lives. Freedom to spend time with people they love, freedom to go after spiritual pursuits, freedom to find happiness. It's possible to find these things in the office, but I personally think it's harder. That said, there are also the practical reasons I list below and in the stories above.

So here are the 10 reasons you need to quit your job right now. And below that I have the methods for doing it. And, by the way, even if you love your job, it always helps to both have a Plan B (nothing is safe) and to also think of yourself as a one-person entrepreneurial business even within the context of your job. It will make the job, more fun, meaningful, and successful.

I. SAFETY. We used to think you get a corporate job, you rise up, you get promoted maybe you move horizontally to another division or a similar company, you get promoted again, and eventually you retire with enough savings in your IRA. That's all gone. That myth disappeared in 2008. It really never existed but now we know it's a myth. Corporate CEOs kept their billion dollar salaries and laid off about 20 million people and sent the jobs to China. Fine, don't complain or blame other people. But your job is not safe.

2. HOME. Everyone thinks they need a safe job so they can save up to buy a home and also qualify for a mortgage. Mortgage lenders at the banks like people who are like them – other people locked in cubicle prison. Well now you don't need to worry about that. We have already discussed why you should never own a home in the first place. Save yourself the stress.

3. COLLEGE. Everyone thinks they need to save up to send their kids to college. Depending on how many kids you have and where you want them to go to college it could cost millions. Well now we know you don't need to send your kid to college. So you don't need to stress about that money anymore.

4. THEIR BOSS. Most people don't like their boss. It's like any relationship only one of the parts has more power from the get-go. Most of the time you get into a relationship for the wrong reasons anyway. Eventually you're unhappy. And if you don't get out, you become miserable and scarred for life.

5. THEIR COWORKERS. See above.

6. FEAR. We have such a high unemployment rate, people are afraid if they leave the job they are miserable at, they won't be able to get a job. This is true if you just walk into your boss's

office and pee on his desk and get fired. But it's not true if you prepare well. More on that in a bit.

7. THE WORK. Most people don't like the work they do. They spend 4 years going to college, another few years in graduate school, and then they think they have to use that law degree, business degree, architecture degree and then guess what? They hate it. But they don't want to admit it. They feel guilty. They are in debt. No problem. Read on.

8. BAD THINGS HAPPEN. Stress, anxiety, bad health, etc all start to happen. You get caught up in the politics and it's only downhill. And it gets worse and worse. You don't want to look back at your life and say, *"man, those were the worst 45 years of my life."* That wouldn't feel good.

9. THE ECONOMY IS ABOUT TO BOOM. I don't care if you believe this or not. Stop reading the newspaper so much. They are trying to scare you. Bernanke just printed up a trillion dollars and airlifted it onto the US economy. Who is going to scoop that up. You in your cubicle? Think.

10. YOUR JOB HAS CLAMPED YOUR CREATIVITY. You do the same thing every day. You want to be jolted, refreshed, and rejuvenated.

*

So: Henry and Aaron asked a good question: you still need to support yourself, you still need to support your family, you can't just walk into your boss's office and quit.

Good point. You need to prepare. It's like training for the Olympics if you feel now is the time to move on from your job. You need to be physically ready, emotionally (don't quit your job and get divorced on the same day for instance), mentally (get your idea muscle in shape) and spiritually all ready.

I get a lot of criticisms from anonymous people in the Yahoo message boards. My wife Claudia begs me, *"Don't look at the message boards unless you talk to me first."* Because she knows I'm an addict.

77

I tell her "ok" but I know I'm going to look. Because that's what addicts do.

I don't mind when people critique me when they've lost, quit, or have been fired from as many jobs as I have. Or lost a home. Tried to raise two kids with almost nothing. Been as desperately unhappy as sometimes I've been. This doesn't qualify me for anything, of course. Maybe it disqualifies me. Who cares? A lot of people have had much worse than me. And I've been very blessed as well.

Sometimes you can build back up. And sometimes you just think, *"How the hell did this happen to me again?"* You can criticize me on Yahoo message boards. My goal in these chapters is to help people maybe think for a split second they can reduce some stress in their lives, they don't have to go through what I went through, they can throw themselves into experience and still come back alive, and at the end of the day, they can use some of these ideas to live a better and more fulfilling life. I've had that experience and I like to write about it.

Much of self-help either deals with the spiritual aspects (how to achieve some sort of happiness through a process they might call "enlightenment") or through physical aspects ("how to make more money," "how to advance in your career," etc.).

But the reality is that we all live on the planet, with families, with aspirations and goals. We don't live in caves and stare at the third eye all day. We can't afford to. We need money to live. We need money for freedom. Understanding how to get that freedom on the outside while we are simultaneously trying to get that freedom on the inside is the true path to happiness.

Getting grounded in our own internal compass and dealing realistically with the world, or as the saying goes: "being in the world but not of it" is what leads us to being fulfilled beings capable of being wealthy, abundant, healthy, and of service to others.

When we get clear about where we individually come from, outside from all brain-washing then we can make decisions that come from wisdom, center, and clear-cut discernment. Then we become humans again.

Phew, this was a hard chapter to write. I did love my job. And it was hard leaving it. But ultimately you outgrow your job and your career can take many directions. I'm tired now. I'm going to force my two kids to watch "Star Wars" whether they like it or not.

What You Need to do if You Were Fired Today

I was brought into the office of the head of the company and he said, *"Your contract is up and we won't be needing you anymore."* I asked. *"Can I stay a few days more to just finish what I was working on?"* And he said, *"No. You need to leave today."* He had thick blonde hair, blue eyes, and a square jaw, was about fifty and looked a little bit like Robert Redford. He smiled at me then. That's the last thing I remember. His smile almost blinded me. I hate him. I was barely put together. I felt like the worst loser. I couldn't understand. I thought I had been doing good work. But suddenly I was damaged goods.

Another time I was... And another time I did... And another and another and another. I've been fired so many times I can't list them all. I can't possibly make you cry over my sorrows because we all have them.

I would pace at three in the morning. *"I'm going to lose this house. My kids are going to switch schools. I have three months to live. I'm going to lose this house. I'm going to this and that and this/that."* The chatter doesn't stop and it's nightmarish at three in the morning. And at four, and at five, and it doesn't stop when the kids wake up and they don't know anything is different but I cry then because everything is different. Because the house is a prison. Because my head is a mental asylum.

No advice helps. You can't meditate. You can't exercise. You can't eat healthy. You can't shave. Or bathe. You can't even take deep breaths. They feel like bullshit breaths. Shit breathes in and shit

79

breathes out. You can't pray or read spiritual texts. None of that stuff helps, you think: None of that immediately deposit's money in the bank. None of that brings back your self-esteem which was so randomly stolen from you by faceless bureaucrats living on the outskirts of cubicles.

So here's advice that helps. I hope you follow it because I know it worked for me:

Do just one thing today.

And then do one thing tomorrow. And the next. That's all. Just one thing a day. If you do your thing, then feel good. You did it! Tomorrow you do the next thing. THAT'S ALL YOU NEED TO DO.

Some preliminaries: First, you need to sleep. Make sure you sleep 8 hours a day, every day. And you can't drink. Delete your news-intake. You don't need news now. Things are bad. But they aren't as bad as they seem. The media lies every day about how bad things are. Trust me.

And then do one solid thing each day.

Here are some possible "one things:"

SCHEDULE a lunch with someone you haven't seen in three years. Could be anyone. But it has to be someone you haven't seen in at least three years. This injects new blood into the system. You need a total transfusion to get rid of the infected old blood.

IDEAS. Find your "customers." Treat yourself like a one-man business. Make a list of customers (i.e. places or people you might want to work with). Then come up with a list of 10 ideas for each customer/place you might want to work. Ideas that can make them money. This way you keep your idea muscle intact. Don't let your idea muscle atrophy! Pitch your ideas to that customer if you can. If you can't move onto the next customer. But wait until tomorrow. You did your thing for today. Be proud. THIS TECHNIQUE WORKS. It has worked for me.

GRATITUDE. Make a list of the people you've worked with over the past ten years that you are grateful you worked with. Email them and tell them why you were grateful you worked with them. Ask them sincerely how they are doing. This is one of the most important things on this list. Why? Because a network increases in value the more nodes it has. Everyone you've ever come into contact with is a node in the network. But many of those nodes have weakened due to lack of care. When you remind them who you are through the sincere gratitude you feel, it strengthens that node. And when a node is strengthened on a network, the value of the network increases exponentially.

WAKE UP early, exercise, take a shower, wear a suit, go into the city, and walk around. Smell that freshness on you. It makes you feel as if you are ready for anything. And you are. That's all you need to do that day. Heck, go to a museum. You won't have this opportunity for freedom forever.

SLASH. Make a list of all expenses you can slash. Make your runway as long as possible. There are plenty of sites to advise how to do this. Actually, even as I write this, I realize there is a BS element to it. A lot of personal finance sites and books recommend this type of activity. But for most people, it's not so easy. Most people don't have a three month runway or even a two week runway. Don't be afraid to drastically change your life. Everything is open. And there's nothing to be ashamed of. Sell your house. Move. Do whatever you can to buy yourself time. Try to do freelance jobs. Very important is to use this time to start doing the DAILY PRACTICE I recommend below. Your life will change but it needs the time to change. Your goal with "Slash" is to buy that time, whatever it costs. Whatever you have to do. You need time. Enough "time" and you have bought yourself freedom.

LUNCH. Have lunch with one person in your industry. Have your ideas ready for that person. Have him critique your ideas. Learn.

RECONNECT. Contact other people who used to work at your old company. Maybe they even worked there ten years ago. Reconnect. Come up with ideas for them.

WRITE. Write a book in the next three days. You can write a 30 page book about dieting ("100 ways to Lose 100 pounds") and put it on sale on Amazon in one day. Why not? The traditional book industry is over. Write the book "100 things to do the day after you are fired." Make it funny. Time to dominate the publishing industry while you are unemployed. Today make a list of all the possible 30 page books you can do. Then tomorrow start one of the books. I have one friend who just self-published a book. He was dead broke before that after being fired from his job. He made $100,000 in 90 days. No joke. This was about a month ago.

RESENTMENT. You are going to feel resentful about people at your old job. They wronged you. But listen closely: they are just trying to survive also. They aren't different from you and me, no matter how much you feel they wronged you. You don't have to love them. But don't waste time hating them. If anything, write them a note thanking them and noting some of their good qualities. This keeps them, in a subtle way, in your network. Worst case (and maybe best case) you never hear from them again.

BRAINSTORM. Go completely in a different direction. What other industry can you work in? What other location can you live in? Make up the wildest fantasies about what you can do. Keep going until there is one possible direction you can execute on today. Brainstorm what blog you can do (and what products you can sell on the blog). Brainstorm about photography (anyone need a photographer this weekend?) Brainstorm about ecommerce (check out penny auction sites where you can buy stuff for pennies and resell on Ebay). I don't know. I'm making stuff up. But brainstorm for an hour and some little slice of reality might peak through.

By the way, if the idea of writing 100 ideas is scaring you, or you don't "feel" like doing it, or you think "it's not for me," realize that you are falling back unconscious into the old paradigm. I suggest that if you catch this happening to you and are determined to become your own person, then come up with 200 ideas. If that scares you even more that is good. You don't want to know what happens if you tell me you rather not write the 200. 300 anyone?

Get out of your own way, which is your old way of thinking. Do something different, shake the internal system, you have the time after all.

Remember: just one thing a day at first. Some of these things above seem crazy. But I'm not recommending anything that I haven't done and made money doing. All of them.

If you are feeling better, go for the full Daily Practice. But don't stress it. The Daily Practice has always worked for me when I've hit my low points on repeated occasions. But first do "one thing a day." No pressures.

And anyone who was fired yesterday, March 10, feel free to call me anytime to chat. Contact me first thru the email on this site, leave me your number, and I will call you. Corporate stability has always been a myth. But entrepreneurship and risk is also a myth. We were never without risk. Risk is life. But now you are forced to embrace it. The good thing is, sometimes embracing leads to love.

What You Need to do if You Were Hired Today

The woman right next to me was alive one second, then a taxi came up on the sidewalk of 42nd Street between 6th and 7th Avenue, hit her and veered off and now the woman was dead. This happened on the first or second day of my work when I started at HBO. I tried to call 911 in the payphone (there were still payphones in August, 1994) and then I had to go. The woman was dead.

And I had to go to work.

I loved HBO like I would love a parent. I wanted them to approve of me. And kiss me as I went to sleep at night.

Before I got the job offer to work there I would watch HBO all day long. My friend Peter and I would watch HBO or MTV for 10 hours straight. I'd go over his house around 1pm in the afternoon and by 10pm we would look at each other and say, *"what the hell did we just do."* Everything from the "the Larry Sanders Show" on HBO to "Beavis & Butthead" on MTV. We couldn't stop. I loved the product. I wanted to work there.

RULE #1: LOVE THE PRODUCT. You have to love the current output of the company. If you work at HBO, love the shows. Watch every single show. No excuses. If you work at WD-40, know every use of WD-40. Make up a few more that nobody ever thought of. If you work at Otis Elevators, understand all the algorithms for how it decides which floors to stop on when. If you work at Goldman Sachs, read every book on the history, study every deal they've done, know Lloyd Blankfein's favorite hobbies and how he rose through the ranks. You have to love the product the way Andre Agassi loves playing tennis or Derek Jeter loves playing baseball.

When I started at HBO I would every day borrow VHS tapes from their library. I watched every show going ten years back. In my spare time I'd stay late and watch TV. I'd watch all the comedians. I even watched the boxing matches that initially made HBO famous. Which leads me to...

RULE #2: KNOW THE HISTORY. When my first company, Reset, was acquired by a company called Xceed, I learned the history of the mini-conglomerate that Xceed was created out of. There was a travel agency for corporations. I visited them in California. There was a burn gel company. I visited them and met all the executives and learned the technical details how the gel was invented. There was a corporate incentives company. I met with them to see if any of their clients could become my clients.

At HBO, I learned how Michael Fuchs (the head of HBO Sports at the time. Later CEO of HBO) in 1975 aired the first boxing match that went out on satellite. And how Jerry Levin (the CEO of HBO, later CEO of Time Warner) used satellites to send the signal out to the cable providers. The first time that had ever happened. Ted Turner had been so inspired by that he turned his local TV affiliate, TBS, into a national TV station, and the rest became history.

Rule #3: Know the history of the executives. At HBO I studied the org chart religiously. My title was "programmer analyst, IT department" and yet I was always asking around: how did John Billock become head of Marketing (he trudged around house to house selling HBO subscriptions in Louisiana when Showtime started up decades earlier). Where did my boss's boss's boss's boss work before arriving at HBO (Pepsi). Where did the head of Original Programming get his start? (He was a standup comedian, later CEO of HBO, before being forced to quit when choking his girlfriend in a Las Vegas parking lot). It was like reading about the origins of all the superheroes. I was a fan-boy and my heroes were the other executives. I wanted to be one of them. Or better.

Know all of your colleagues and what their dreams and ambitions are. Get to work 2 hours before they get to work. If they need favors, do them. You have a whole two hours extra a day. You can do anything.

Rule #4: Make your boss look good. Your entire job in life is to make your boss look good. You don't care about yourself. You only want your boss to get promotions, raises, etc. Remember, you can never make more than your boss. So the more he makes, the better he does, the better you will do. It's the only way to rise up. Work hard, give him full credit for everything you do. Don't take an ounce of credit. At the end of the day, everyone knows where credit belongs. But even then, thank him for everything and direct all credit back to him (or her). Here's how you make your boss look good:

- **Get to work two hours before him.** If that means you have to wake up and go in at 5am then do it. Two extra hours of work a day is an extra 500 hours of work a year. None of your co-workers can compete with that.

- **Walk with him to his car, train, etc.** when he leaves work. You need to know his goals, his initiatives, his plans, his family troubles, etc. Of course, no stalking. But the relationship will grow over time if you keep planting the seeds for it.

- AND, AGAIN, GIVE HIM FULL CREDIT FOR EVERYTHING. And thank him regularly for the opportunity to do the work you are doing.

- Come up with 10 ideas to improve the current situation (don't cause more work for other employees, just get creative, give him something he needs)

- Anticipate something that may be stressing her out, propose solutions BEFORE he or she asks.

- Pay attention to cues, notice when she or he wants you to stop talking.

- Take notes when talking to her or him, email her lists of the agreements of what you do, do everything and more, make it clear – yet subtle – that you are over delivering in every front.

RULE #5: KNOW ALL THE SECRETARIES. It may be a cliché but the secretaries run the company. They control all of the schedules. They dish out all of the favors. Take as many secretaries out to lunch as possible. Not just in your department but in every department. Particularly HR. HR knows all of the gossip. Knows everything that is happening. It's not so hard to do this. First off, HR gives you all of your intro material when you join the company. Ask those people out to lunch after you've settled in for a few weeks. If someone writes an internal company newsletter, ask that person to lunch. Ask your boss's boss's boss's boss's secretary out to lunch. Nobody will think you are going over their head. You're asking to lunch "just" a secretary. This was invaluable to me at every company I've ever worked at.

RULE #6: CONSTANTLY TEST YOUR VALUE ON THE MARKET. The job market is like any other market. There's supply and demand. And you're just an item for sale at the great bazaar. Every year you need to find out what your value is on the market. For one thing, the best way to get an increase in salary and status is to move horizontally, not vertically. Second, you don't want to get inbred. A good friend of mine was in HBO's marketing department for 17 years. I set up a dinner between her, me, and the CEO of an advertising agency that was hiring. The CEO was one of my closest friends. Still, she couldn't hire my HBO friend. *"She's too inbred,"* she said. *"She will never be able to get the HBO way of doing things out of her head."*

When I was at HBO I was constantly talking to people at other companies. I had lunch with top people at Showtime. I knew people from all the other divisions of Time Warner. I was always asking people to lunch of breakfast. I would get offers from the banking industry. I would try to work within different divisions of HBO. Everytime I got another offer, I got another raise and promotion at HBO. Sometimes substantial (up to 35% increases). My bosses would resent me for it, but then go back to "Rule #4" and often they would get raises also.

By the way, if you ask someone to lunch, why would they say yes? Often I would do it under the guise of either, *"I'd like to ask you for advice"* or *"I have ideas for you."* It's hard for people to say "no" to either of those. Promise you will keep it short, and stick to it. One hour. And if they do, then they aren't the right contact for you at this time. Don't ask the CEO of a major company. But move up the chain.

RULE #7: STUDY ALL THE MARKETING CAMPAIGNS. In 1996 they switched their slogan to "It's not TV. It's HBO." That slogan lasted for 13 years. Before that it was "Simply the Best," then "Something Special's On." When they switched to "It's not TV," Eric Kessler, the head of marketing, gave a talk on how they came up with the slogan. All his employees were in the auditorium. And me from the IT department. Nobody else would go with me. I knew every slogan HBO ever had.

RULE #8: STUDY THE INDUSTRY. What made HBO different from Showtime. From Cinemax? From non-pay cable? From broadcasting. I ready every book about the history of TV I could find. I would go to lectures at the Museum of Radio and Television on 52nd Street (the best was a day that members of the MTV show "The Real World" gave a panel. After the panel I followed one group of other people in the audience for 30 blocks while they talked about the panel and the show. I wanted to break in so many times. They would be my new best friends. We would have parties around showings of "The Real World." But I was too shy and eventually they all split off in different directions, leaving me alone). Jessica Reif Cohen was the Merrill analyst covering media. I knew nothing about stocks. But I read everything she wrote and would scan the WSJ for mentions of her name.

When I was trying to sell my first company, Reset. I called every company in the industry. Omnicom, Razorfish, Agency.com, etc etc. I read every SEC filing so I would know the nuances of all their deals and financings. When I was building Stockpickr I became obsessed with the mechanics of how Yahoo Finance worked and the ways in which she (Yahoo Finance is a "she," and I love her) delivered traffic to all of her media sources. With HBO it was fascinating to me because at one point the CEOs of Showtime, Time Warner, Universal, Viacom, Fox Sports, etc were all former executives at HBO.

RULE #9: BECOME THE COMPANY. I was a lowly programmer in the IT department. We were so far from the normal business operations of the company that they even put us in a different building. But that didn't matter to me. I WAS HBO. That was my mantra. I became so absorbed in every aspect of the company that I knew that any idea I had would be a good idea for the company. At least I felt this (not sure if anyone else did). I never said, "I think this," I said, "We should do this." HBO and I were a "We." Inseparable.

Until you have that feeling of unity with the company you work for, you can't rise up. Key, though: when you have an idea, make sure you know how to execute the idea also. In detail. Ideas are a dime a dozen. And execution is worth a million dollars. And I mean that specifically, if you execute on a good idea, you'll make a million dollars or more from it.

RULE #10. LEAVE. All good things must come to an end. From the day you start, you need to plan your exit. Not like in rule #6, "Know Your Value" where you are trying to figure out your corporate salary value. "Leave" means something different. It means you're going to say goodbye forever.

If you master Rules #1-9 at a company then you'll know enough about the company and industry to start your own company. To either become a competitor or a service provider. And you will have built in customers because your rolodex will be filled with people from the industry. If you constantly think like an entrepreneur from the instant you walk into your cubicle on day one of your job then you will constantly looking for those missing gaps you can fill. This is how you jump into the abyss. You make sure the abyss has a customer waiting for you.

I did everything wrong my first few months at HBO. I didn't know NYC. I didn't know corporate culture at all. I wore the same suit five days in a row until I realized nobody else was wearing a suit and I never wore one again. I didn't have the requisite skill set to survive at my job (they had to send me to a remedial programming school despite the fact that I had majored in programming AND went to graduate school for computer science).

I was obsessed with the Internet and HBO didn't even own HBO.com at the time. My boss's boss's boss would say to my boss, *"get him away from that Internet stuff and onto some real work."* One time my boss came into my cubicle and with everyone listening from every other cubicle said to me, *"we want you to succeed here but you need to know more or else it's not going to work out."* It was very embarrassing and nobody around me would meet my eyes for the next week or so. I was the walking dead. I was sure I was going to get fired every day.

But I survived then. And every day since.

Nobody Cares About You But You

People got educated after the dot-com boom. A lot of people realized that they needed to start separating from the corporate myth and become their own "personal brand." Suddenly that was the hot phrase: "are you branding yourself?" like you were a cow that needed your own unique mark in order to stand out.

There are three layers to this discussion:

There's the real you. Who knows what that is.

There's the branded you. The appearance you want to have for the outside world. Are you the "eccentric genius" or are you "the guy who gets things done" or the "social media expert," etc.

There's the actual branding. i.e. what are you doing to get the brand out there: Facebook, Twitter, blogging, etc.

I'm not making fun of any of this. The notion of branding is real. But I would try as much as possible to blend "A" and "B".

In 1995 I was reading about popular websites. Unfortunately I forget the exact website but there was a girl putting her diary online (a blog!). One unique aspect of this girl was that she had a severe case of chronic fatigue syndrome. She slept for 20 hours a day. She was 15. Then she would put her thoughts and feelings (and depression) about it online. Her site, at that time, was more popular than People Magazine's website.

What impressed me about that is that honest, sincere voices will always rise to the top. When you are fearless and fierce, you will shine.

To me, the word "branding" comes across as "lying". As in, "here's what my product really is, but now I'm going to try and convince you that my product is something special, something "new!" and exciting.

And then I'm going to use various tricks to convince you of this.

How much easier is it if you don't have to lie and then you don't have to do any tricks? You just be yourself.

Well, you can ask, what if that is not enough to get me noticed. No problem, I would answer, just keep improving yourself.

The robots aren't improving themselves. They get their programming and then they live their mechanical lives every day. I don't hate them. It's just reality.

By the way "improve yourself" is sort of a bogus self-help term. I don't like it. The phrase "your self" is unclear. We don't know who "your self" is yet. You might have just gotten out of Corporate America. You might be still dealing with all the brainwashing. You might still be dealing with the nuclear aftermath of a relationship gone bad. But I'll use the phrase "improve yourself" as a start. In this context it means, getting rid of the programming of the Zombie Recruitment Machine, following the Daily Practice outlined in the chapter below, and really beginning the next phase of your life. "Improve yourself" can easily be reworded as "beginning yourself."

So if you actively attempt to improve yourself, then that improvement compounds exponentially. Every day, the "real you" (and, again, whatever that means) starts to make itself heard. You might need help doing this. People need to call "bullshit" on you and you have to know who to listen to and who to tune out. Subsequent chapters in this book will help with that, as well as how to become the "better" you.

Every day, I fight my internal battles. And every day the front lines move a little bit further. A little bit further to where? I don't know. But I'm sure I will tell you when I get there.

And how will I tell you? Easy, I'll blog about it and write a book about it and tweet about it and do whatever else I can. Because I like doing that. I like being honest with people and sharing my experiences.

I self-published a book. "How to Be the Luckiest Person Alive." I published it in paperback form, kindle form, and free PDF (see directions below to get free PDF). The entire process took me three weeks.

Using an established publisher would've taken over a year.

See the below chapter on the prior sales of my five other books, all published with traditional publishers. (Also, including a part about how my wife finally fell for me). But I'm never going to publish in the morgue of the publishing industry again. THIS CHAPTER IS ABOUT WHY I DID IT AND HOW YOU CAN DO IT.

The book publishing industry is dead and they don't know it. It's like how the typewriter industry died. And how companies like Blockbuster and Borders can't survive. And the entire music industry is dying. And broadcast television might be on the way. And the tablet industry is the first sign that companies like DELL might be in major trouble. And companies like Sirius mean the radio industry is dead.

Why did I self-publish?

Advances are quickly going to zero. Margins are going to zero for publishers. There's no financial benefit for going with a publisher if advances are going to zero and royalties are a few percentage points. The publishing industry does minimal editing. The time between book acceptance and release is too long (often a year or more). That's insane and makes zero sense in a print-on-demand world when kindle versions are outselling print versions.

Most importantly, the book industry sells "books." What they need to do is sell their "authors." Authors now are brands, they are businesses, they are mini-empires. Publishers do nothing to help 95% of their authors build their platforms and their own brands. This would increase author loyalty and make the lack of a meaningful advance almost worth it. As a side note: 12 million typewriters sold in 1950. 400,000 in 2009.

I'll give you a quick example. I've published five books with major publishers. The majority of books now are sold through Amazon. Not a single publisher told me I can log into Amazon Author Central, create an author's page, link my author's page to my BLOG, upload a VIDEO, have my TWITTER feed in there, have an FAQ in there, and all the other basic tools Amazon uses to market your book. Why? This is the world's biggest bookseller. Why wasn't I told about a basic marketing platform I could use? I just learned about it as I prepared to self-publish, after writing books the traditional route for eight years. Now I have it all hooked up and I have a feeling I've only begun to explore the Author Central area and what Amazon can do for me.

I don't want to trash the publishers. In the chapter after this one I detail my experiences with publishers and reveal my complete sales numbers, etc. I completely open every kimono (and it's pretty hideous inside that kimono). They are all hard working people and have done good jobs but it's just not worth it to me to go that way anymore.

Despite my five books I am sure zero publishers would've ever published "How to Be the Luckiest Person Alive!" It's not in my finance core.

Publishers, just like in any business, put you in your little corner and you have to stay there. They want to pigeon-hole you. If you try to get up and go to a different corner they slap you down. So publishers would ignore the topic of my book, despite the popularity of my blog which I would be able to demonstrate to them with statistics. The statistics show that the less I spoke about finance, the more popular my blog got. People want more happiness, not more ways they can lose their money reading bullshit.

I recently looked at the Bookscan (the "Nielsen ratings" of the book industry, Bookscan informs all the editors how many books of every title are sold each week) numbers for a bunch of very well-known finance authors. They were all close to zero. Plus, in the link above I reveal all my numbers on my books. Again, almost nothing. Know why? Because people know that reading these books won't do anything for them. Very few people make money on stocks. The stock market is largely a scam. Nobody makes money owning real estate anymore. Personal finance is a joke with zero percent interest rates. And, to be honest, most self-help books are written by people with no experience and are just filled with meaningless platitudes.

Thinking about finance is the opposite of the true goal, which is being happy. In this book, I talk about my many failures. Going dead broke after making millions. Rising from the gutter. Getting fired from jobs, kicked out of school, losing a marriage, being at a crossroads in life and figuring out which way to go, and all the times where I could've used a book like this to figure out how to grow from the core inward to find happiness, success, and the other tools I needed to come out of the hole and find the motivation to achieve some good for both myself and the world.

This book describes that and the specific techniques I used. I'm brutally honest, to the point of risking people hating me. I've lost friends (at least temporarily) over the material in this book.

But so what? It works. It worked for me. It's worked for others in huge, almost unbelievable ways. I feel real, like a human again.

And I'm willing to bet not a single publisher would've touched it. Nor would they have been able to get it out as fast as I could and as cheaply as I could. I don't care about making money on this book. I don't need to feed an entire corporate establishment. I want the ideas out there so I can help people.

Honestly, I'm also selfish. I want my the ideas out there so my name gets out there a bit more. This won't be my last book. I have 10 more on the way!

And so do you!

Here's what I did to self-publish.

- I created an account on createspace.com. They are owned by Amazon. Great customer service. You have any question at all you hit a button that says "Call Me" and within 30 seconds they have a customer representative calling your phone.

- I downloaded a Microsoft Word template they provided. This template took into account whether a page was a left page or a right page, it helped build the table of contents, kept the page numbers accurate, etc. In other words, the template used by any publisher in the world when they format your book.

- I made a cover. Createspace had over a million options when you combined their templates with images, fonts, etc. I used one of their photos. Claudia used a photo I took, uploaded it and made her book, *"21 Things to Know Before Starting an Ashtanga Yoga Practice."* 160 pages or so. My book is 166 pages.

- I saved it as a PDF and uploaded it. I let them pick the ISBN number.

- I picked a price of $7.95 for the book. This was the minimum price I could go if I wanted them to distribute it to bookstores, libraries, etc. along with Amazon. I get about a $2 royalty per book at that price. But if you chose a price of $20 then you would get about a $14 royalty. Much higher than any publisher will ever give you. I chose a low price because I'm trying to get as many copies out as possible. I have many books to go and want the audience to be happier and happier with each product. Personally, I would prefer if you get the free book – directions below to get it.

- They sent a proof. I liked it. Once I approved of the proof it was officially published at createspace.com. About two days later it was on Amazon.com.

- I hit a button to format it as a Kindle book. Up until now everything was free but formatting for the kindle requires some work. That cost me $69. Three weeks later they sent me the documents formatted for kindle and I had to use Amazon Author Central to upload the kindle version. Again, I priced it as low as they would let me. $0.99. Within 48 hours it was on Amazon.

- I also created my Amazon page, linked the RSS feed of my blog to it, created a video and uploaded it, linked my twitter feed to it, etc.

- FREE: I'm giving out my previous book free (the PDF, which basically looks like the Kindle version).

HERE'S THE DIRECTIONS TO GET A FREE VERSION:

Email this address: LuckiestPersonAlive@gmail.com

The subject line has to be: "Luckiest Person Alive Free Book"

You'll get an email within seconds. There won't be an attachment but there will be a link to the full PDF on Google Docs. You can read it as a PDF there. Or If you want it also as an attachment you can then click "Share" on the right and email it to yourself (or whomever) as an attachment. All for free.

That's all you need to do. I would encourage every author in the world to start doing this. Like with any medium, the true, sincere, honest voices will rise to the top. Hopefully the entertaining ones as well. I think anything I put out there will be both. If you have any questions or concerns about this entire process, email me through my blog: jamesaltucher.com.

I obvious have no self-interest by creating competitors. The more people who publish in a graveyard, the better it is for me. But I honestly want you to publish your ideas and words.

We'll all do this together.

Why I Write Books

Even Though I've Lost Money on Every Book I've Written

I had two kids, a house that I couldn't sell (it was right next to "Ground Zero" in NYC), I was almost broke, and my monthly burn killing me. I lost track. I was going to go broke and then probably kill myself. I wouldn't be able to afford diapers and food for my 2 month old baby. Two years earlier, to the day, I looked at my bank statement and I had about $15,000,000 in there. At that time, late 2001, almost nothing.

I wrote some software to trade with what little money I had left.

For 12 months in a row, with the market going straight down (Enron imploding, Worldcom imploding, Tyco imploding, etc.) I used signals generated by the software I had written in late 2001 to buy stocks (I only bought, never shorted) and I made my monthly nut. On days when I lost money I would cry. I saw my bank account going to zero. I had a life insurance policy so I figured I could kill myself in the worst case and my family would be able to live on the four million that would result. I tried to figure out ways I could kill myself where nobody would know it was a suicide. But I didn't want it to come to that.

So I figured out how to trade. Or my software figured out how to trade. And I started trading for other people and taking a percentage of the profits. I was making my monthly burn.

So I wrote a book. It came out in mid-2004. Back then I was trading my software successfully for about five different hedge funds or individuals (for example Victor Niederhoffer). *"Trade Like a Hedge Fund"* was the book. Pamela van Giessen from Wiley, who had published Victor Niederhoffer's book, was the editor. She had really encouraged me. I wanted to write about things that people should avoid in the market. She said no, people want positive stuff. She said, specifically, call it *"Trade Like a Hedge Fund"* and write about all your techniques that work. So I did.

She gave me an advance. $5000. When the book came out, Niederhoffer hated it. I was up over 100% for him in the prior year He thought I was giving away all his techniques even though he only traded futures and all my signals in the book were for stocks and were signals I had been trading long before I met him. He wrote me an email, "YOU ARE A TOTAL LAUGHING STOCK." I felt horrible because I looked up to him so much. He trashed me and the book on his email list. People who had been my friends stopped talking to me on blind faith.

It was the best thing that could've happened. The book became controversial and became my bestselling book. Barrons had it as one of their books of the year. The Stock Trader's Almanac had it as THE book of the year for 2004. I started giving talks for Fidelity about the techniques in the book. I called Pamela the other day. *"How many books did that one sell,"* 14,074 copies.

That's it. And that was a best seller (for finance books). I still get an occasional royalty check from that one. I think $300 was my last. I probably pulled about $25,000 total from it. Maybe a bit more.

Pamela and I decided to work on my next book. I wanted to do something on Warren Buffett. How he was a more active trader than anyone believed. *"Do 'Trade Like Warren Buffet',"* she said. So I did. My advance: $7500.

A book is brutal. It's the worst thing. You do nothing for about 3-6 months while you write it and all the time you are saying, *"why did I agree to write this. I am never going to write a book again."* The book came out. Complete failure. Pamela told me the other day that in total 6552 copies were sold. It came out six years ago. I thought the religion of Buffett would've kicked in at some point and his followers would've bought the book. But the religion has him as the prophet of value investing and I was saying he wasn't. Blasphemy!

So I did another book. Because I needed to reclaim the positive feelings I felt when my first book sold over 10,000 copies. I loved the book "Supermoney" by Adam Smith, written in the early 70s. Pop finance at its best. In the book, he meets a young retired investor who had called it quit's with twenty million cash in the bank and was trying to figure out what to do with his life. That young investor was Warren Buffett. Every chapter had a surprise like that.

So I wrote "Supercash" about hedge fund strategies. This time, to Pamela's surprise, I got an agent. My advance: $30,000. The book is horrible. I can't even open it. Here, right now as I write this I am taking the book off the bookshelf and throwing it in the garbage. I think I even signed this book. It sold 1565 copies.

Then the stock market went on fire. And with Stockpickr, a site my business partner, Dan, and I built in late 2006 (and sold to thestreet.com in 2007), I had a built-in audience of a million people. So I decided to do another book. Pam couldn't buy it. I was a failure now at Wiley so they passed. Penguin picked it up. I forget the exact advance now but it was somewhere between $80,000-$100,000. If I ever told you it was more than that, I probably lied on purpose.

The book was set for publication in December, 2008. I BEGGED THEM TO WAIT. Nobody was going to buy a book about stocks called "The Forever Portfolio" in the worst bear market in history. Nobody.

But they had to do it. It was on the schedule. I had written the book almost a year earlier. The world had been different. But this is why book publishing in the finance space in particular is going to slowly disappear. Ebooks and ebook publishers will take down every single traditional finance book publisher. It's inevitable.

SO THE BOOK FLOPPED. The publisher would barely return my calls. In total it sold 1598 copies. All my other books had been priced from $40-70 but I wanted to do a cheap one so this was priced around $20. But it still flopped. People were worried whether or not they were going to survive. Not what stocks they should buy for "Forever". The goddamn stock market was going down 300 points a day.

I went around to every bookstore in the city. I would write notes on the inside of every book and then put them back on the bookshelf. Things like, *"if you buy this book you will make a billion dollars"* Or, *"you are the smartest person in the world for buying this book."*

One time, at a random mega book store in the city, with my daughter Mollie looking on, I wrote, "I LOVE YOU" in the inside of the book. *"Daddy!"* she said, *"what the heck are you doing?"* But still the book flopped. Nobody loved me back.

One time, a friend of mine was pitching the same publisher a book. I don't know who she was talking to. They didn't know she knew me. She asked them: *"What did you do to market James Altucher's book."* They said: *"We got him a review in the Financial Times, an excerpt published in thestreet.com, and we got him on CNBC."* She called me right afterward and told me this and we both laughed.

I wrote my own review in the FT! I was at thestreet.com and got the excerpt there. And I had been doing a weekly spot on CNBC for years and talked my own book there.

So I wanted to write another book, even though I'VE HATED THE PROCESS OF WRITING EVERY SINGLE BOOK I'VE EVER WRITTEN. My agent called Penguin. They didn't want it. I actually think they personally hated me (not even a courtesy call to me when they rejected it). I didn't even approach Pamela. I was too ashamed that I had jilted her for Penguin so I could get the higher advance. I told my agent who I wanted to do the book with. In fact, the exact editor I wanted to do the book with.

He sent the 60 page book proposal (it was the first time I ever had to write an actual proposal) to 20 editors including the one I specifically wanted to work with, HH at Harper Collins. I was writing for the WSJ then, doing other stuff for News Corp, and I thought it would be a perfect fit for her given the books I saw that she had edited. Other writers had told me she was great to work with. I had done my research.

She rejected it.

I called my agent and said, *"This is a mistake. This book is perfect for her. Please do this: call her and take her out to lunch. Find out why she rejected it. Explain why it would be a good book with Harper Collins."* All 20 editors he sent to rejected the book. I was convinced not only it was a good idea but a GREAT idea. I kept saying to my agent, *"call back that one editor and take her to lunch or dinner. You need to wine and dine people. You need to at least find out why they are rejecting the book. That's sales. It is information, it is friendship, it is relationships."*

He called me back one time. We had known each other forever but had never had an issue where someone didn't want one of my books. So now I saw what happened when someone didn't want one of my books. *"If you are going to tell me how to do my job,"* he said, *"this relationship is over."* I mumbled an apology and he hung up.

So I wrote an email to HH and explained why the book would be good for her. She agreed to meet me. She said to me, *"this proposal seems like it was written by wikipedia. You need to give us a real methodology for what to do when the end of the world hit's."* I went back home. Wikipedia was still on the screen. I clicked it away and wrote another book proposal. She still didn't really like it. The ideas were great, she said, but she didn't really like the writing. And I agreed with her. I wasn't finding my voice with this one even though I did think the ideas were good.

The WSJ stepped in. RD who runs their books department. She thought it was a great idea for a book so the WSJ bought it, HH and Harper agreed to edit it but Roe found an excellent co-author, Doug Sease, who had been at the newspaper for about 800 years and was now fishing off the coast of Florida. He's the most relaxed guy I ever met. We got the deal with Hollis and split the advance that the WSJ gave us. I can't say what it is because I want to respect Doug's privacy. He would write the intros to each chapter. I would write the ideas, etc., and he would sew it all up. The book was called: *"The Wall Street Journal Guide to Investing for the Apocalypse."*

The basic idea: the media tries to SCARE you every week with a new horror story: PANDEMICS, GLOBAL WARMING, NUCLEAR TERRORISM, RIOTS IN EGYPT. The book is about every way the world could end, and how to make as much money as possible off of these impending apocalypses. The book's been out a few days.

Net-net I've lost money and time from books.

In May, 2009, I had just started dating someone. It was our fourth date and she was going to meet me at the Penn Station book store and then we would take a train to her house and she was going to cook dinner. While she was waiting for me she randomly saw my book, *"The Forever Portfolio"* for sale. She opened it. IT WAS THE SAME UNSOLD BOOK where three months earlier I had written "I LOVE YOU" on the inside. She looked around and thought maybe I had planted it there somehow and was secretly watching her. But I was late to meet her that day. She looked at the inscription again. *"I love you."* A little over a year later we got married. And that's why I write books.

25 Dates Until I Met Claudia

(or, how to cut losses quickly and treat "finding romance" the same way you would treat finding success in any path)

I was on one of my first dates after I had separated from my wife and the girl asked straight out what my net worth was within five minutes of sitting down. I had met the girl in an elevator the night before. I was walking into a building to visit another woman. I noticed this girl and I prayed to God that she would enter the elevator with me. She did. She hit floor #9. I hit floor #10. God is good.

Somewhere around the fourth floor she turned to me and said, *"please tell me 2009 is going to be better than 2008."* She was about five feet tall and had thick blonde hair, light blue eyes. I told her it definitely was. 2008 was bad for everyone in every way. It couldn't get worse. It was horrible for me, I said. I had gotten separated. A month earlier I had been on the floor in a fetal position and then put ads on Craigslist pretending to be a psychic. In my "psychic" capacity I told the future to about 20 different people. And probably tried to hit on ten of them.

I got off the elevator on her floor instead of the tenth floor. We talked for ten minutes. My phone kept ringing. My friend on the tenth floor (a woman) wanted to know where I was since the doorman had announced my presence about fifteen minutes earlier. Somewhere Between the first and tenth floor I got lost in a maze it would take me two months to exit.

My new friend's father had died during the year. And her husband, twenty years older, had cheated on her and divorced her that year. She was crying. She asked where I lived. I said, "The Chelsea Hotel". She said, *"I've never had sex in the Chelsea Hotel."*

My phone kept ringing while we were talking. *"Who is that?"* she said. And I said it was a girl who lived on the tenth floor. So I had to go.

The next day I sent her flowers and a teddy bear. I called her and we agreed to go to dinner.

Right away she asked me my net worth, what the specific details of my divorce were going to be, why wasn't I working, what were my plans for the future, what political party I was a member of, everything. I told her what I had going on. She was skeptical. She said: *"Those sorts of things never work out."* She asked me a million questions. I was honest about everything. She said, *"I didn't think you were a good looking guy last night."* Welcome to New York dating post-marriage.

Her conclusion: "you're completely insane. I can't go out with you." We went out for two months but she broke up with me at least once a week. It was really painful. I didn't have enough self-confidence to stay broken up. She'd break up with me in the morning and then call me later and say, *"let's go out for a drink"* and I would drop all other plans to go out with her again. I was drinking non-stop.

During this time, thestreet.com wanted to "rework" my contract, which resulted in me getting fired two years after I sold Stockpickr to them. The Financial Times lost their advertiser for the page I was writing on so they effectively fired me. CNBC no longer needed a bullish guy when the stock market was going down every day so they stopped using me. I let one business fail and started another business that was doomed to fail. [See Chapters below about these failures]. I invested in a few other businesses but I had no idea then what would happen to those.

And still I kept getting broken up with at least once a week if not more.

My kids would come over every other weekend but since this girl would break up with me every Friday I had no idea what she was doing on a Saturday night and I'd get anxious about it. I'd arrange for my kids to get their nails done or something and I'd try calling this girl but no pickup.

I stopped returning calls from co-investors and my business partner, Dan, had to explain I was sick or busy, or dealing with divorce, or whatever he did to explain to people. None of my friends wanted to meet this new girl because they were all 100% sure that it would not work out.

I started meeting other girls via dating services to fill in the gaps when the first girl would break up with me. One girl was the host of her own TV show on ABC. Her dog shit on my rug. She wanted me to only wear suits. She wanted my teeth whitened. She wanted my hair cropped close to head (ugh!) *"I've written a book on dating,"* she said, *"so you have to have a certain look or else I can't be seen with you."* *"You need to be groomed,"* she said. It didn't work out. Anyone who looks at me can see I can't be groomed even if I wanted to. And being groomed like a dog is hard work!

Another girl asked me: *"How do you deal with all the girls who want you for your millions?"* And I was like, *"I'm not sure where you're getting your information from but it's not what you think."*

That didn't work out. She wrote me a letter at the end (two weeks later), *"you have mental problems and should see someone about that."* She was a psychiatrist so she was an expert. She had said to me a week earlier, *"If you use Ikea to buy furniture for your new apartment I'm going to have to break up with you."* She had to break up with me.

Another girl I introduced to some of my friends. People I had been friends with for about ten years. During the evening she got so drunk her breasts kept falling out of her dress and she wouldn't notice at all. She would keep talking with her breasts fully out of her dress and people at all the other tables looking at us. So I walked her home. On the way back to her place she kept laughing and saying, *"your friends really hate you. They only like you because they don't know who you really are."* I got her into her apartment, dropped her on her bed, and then left and I still think about what she said and wonder if she was right.

I moved into a two bedroom apartment so my kids could visit me. The last time they had visited me in the Chelsea Hotel I saw a used condom on the staircase of the hotel. Not a good environment for kids. The new apartment, right on Wall Street, had a bed for me, two beds for the kids, a couch in the living room, a table but no chairs and no other furniture. The kids and I would keep our clothes on the floor. We'd eat on the floor. We played Monopoly all day long on the floor. By the time they left each weekend the floor was covered with food, games, books, videos, dolls, hairbrushes, whatever.

Then I'd see my friend again on Mondays and she'd break up with me on Tuesday.

I was exhausted of being broken up with. I was broken.

Dating again felt like I had returned from outer space after a 12 year visit around the planet Mars. But the planet had undergone a nuclear war and everyone was radioactive so I couldn't touch them. *"Isn't there anyone out there who isn't radioactive?"* I would ask out loud. But I had nobody to talk to. My apartment was empty. My day was empty. I'd walk around doing nothing.

I finally decided to take it seriously. No more second dates if I knew there was no serious relationship. No more drinking. Back to the Daily Practice for the first time in three years.

I defined for myself very clearly what I wanted. I liked being married. I wanted to meet someone I would marry. But more than that, I wanted a real, committed relationship, one in which we would all look out for the best interests of the other, one where each of us would tend to the fire of the other's soul, a real partner, a best friend. I'm an ugly guy and had no prospects in life at that moment so not the easiest thing.

So my key was: I would treat this like I would treat any job: devote serious time and research to it. Cut losses if things weren't moving towards my goals (e.g. not have sex just because it was there because there are always consequences if no long-term relationship was in the cards since that was my goal). Find someone who had similar values to me in terms of "no game-playing in romance," similar spiritual values, similar flexibility, wouldn't mind (would even love) that I had kids, etc.

It was a fulltime job for me. I spent three or four hours a day writing girls on various dating services. I wanted to meet someone. Finally there was a girl who had an interesting picture who said she was from Buenos Aires. This was on J-Date, a dating site for Jewish people. She was clearly not Jewish. I wrote to her and said she seemed really different. Maybe we could meet for dinner?

She said: *"No dinner. Just tea."* I wanted to push for dinner. Maybe something could happen.

"No. Tea!"

She was from Buenos Aires. I wrote and said, "Oh, I've always wanted to go to Brazil."

She wrote back and said, *"That's nice that you want to go to Brazil but Buenos Aires is in Argentina. They speak Portuguese in Brazil."*

South America is all the same to me. Seems my college education was not coming handy.

We met for tea early in the afternoon one day. She told me she was into yoga and that's what she mostly thought about. She told me all the benefits she felt yoga had. How it was a spiritual discipline as well a physical one. She told me she would take me to yoga and I laughed and said: *"Maybe next lifetime."*

I told her how when I was a kid I was obsessed with trying to have psychic powers to see naked girls. She laughed. I told her I had two kids. She asked me what were their names. I told her how depressed I had been in my worst moments years earlier. She told me her stories. We talked for a long time and it was nice.

We took a walk and sat down on a park bench in Tompkins Square Park. We didn't say anything to each other. We had already run out of topics to talk about. There was nothing but silence until she had to go. But I felt calm. It had been a very long time since I had felt calm. We must have sat like that in silence for about fifteen minutes. It's hard to sit in silence with someone but it wasn't hard this time.

Eventually she got up to go. She had to catch a train. While she was walking to the train she told me she was selling her house. I asked her where she was going to move. She said: *"Maybe the East Village."*

"No you aren't," I thought to myself. *"You're going to move to the corner of Wall Street and Broad. Where I live."* We have just had our first year wedding anniversary.

Success is
a Sexually Contagious Disease

I was having breakfast with a friend mine: call him "Tony." The day before, Tony was having breakfast with a guy I will call T.T., the CEO of "BlackNose," a mega private equity firm. T is known for his extravagant parties at the peak of the housing bubble when his firm was going public. He's worth about $3 billion.

"Tony" said to me, *"the entire breakfast, all TT could talk about was Larry Page from Google. He kept saying, 'that ******g kid is worth $18 billion and I'm only worth $3 billion. How is that even possible? What the hell did he ever do?'"*

Tony, who himself is worth about $100 million said, *"can you believe that? He's worth $3 billion and all can be is angry at Larry Page for having $18 billion. I hope when I have $3 billion I'm not a greedy bustard like that."*

Are Tony and TT successful? Sometimes we lose track of what money is for. It's for freedom. So we have enough to pursue the things that can make us healthy, help keep our minds sharp, and our spiritual lives fulfilled.

Is TT successful just for having $3 billion?

Continually asking the question, "who am I?" boils down the essence of success. Am I the sort of person who needs a private plane to be happy? Or do I need to be VP of a corporation? Or do I need enough to just feed my kids and myself day by day and make sure there is a little set aside for a rainy day? Or do I want to figure out the nature of who I really am and, starting from there, find my success?

There's a story about Joseph Heller, the author of Catch-22, one of my favorite books.

He was at a party in the Hamptons with all sorts of hedge fund managers. One guy came up to him and pointed out a successful

30 year old hedge fund manager. Heller at this time was retired and in his 60s or 70s. I forget. The guy said to him, *"see that 30 year old over there? He makes more in a month than all of your book sales have made for you in your entire lifetime."*

I don't know what Joseph Heller felt when he heard that. Envious? Angry at the person for pointing out such a gross difference? I would've felt a little bit of both to be honest.

But Heller responded, *"But I know one thing I have that he will never have."*

The guy laughed, *"what could that be?"*

Heller responded, *"Enough."*

So everyone has their different definitions of success. There's Heller. There's the hedge fund manager.

There's also the young man or woman of 18 years old who just needs to know, *"yes, I can do it. I can carve my name on this world. I can conquer the world before it conquers me."* I respect that desire. Sometimes you don't want to be silent at the age of 16 for the rest of your life. Sometimes you want to stand on the mountain and shout your name as loud as possible and for many people as possible to hear.

And sometimes you just want to know that you can do it, even if you end up not doing it.

Like I said: lots of definitions of success.

The key for me is this: throw out your definition of success. Again, whatever that definition is: it's probably the result of the massive programming we get from our masters: our parents and first teachers, our friends, our first lovers (since we want to please them), our first bosses and colleagues. And then ever after, we have to decide if we're going to continue to battle the forces of nature to constantly please these false masters, or if we are going to carve our own definition.

How do we carve our own definition? By working from the inside out. Starting from the inside, a natural definition will occur to us.

First, by sticking with traditional definitions (the outside in, rather than the inside out), what pains can happen?

And when I say it's a contagious, sexually transmitted disease – just to remove all doubt – I DON'T MEAN THIS IN A GOOD WAY. It's not like the pseudo self-help advice you see everywhere: *"if you hang out with successful people then you will be successful."* I mean it in a negative way. I meant that the negative effects of success will grow, tumor-like in your brain and body and you'll pass them on to the people around you, the people closest to you. Even your children. And they will be stuck with the disease. And probably die of it. Since, in most cases, it's terminal.

Success is a contagious disease. By the way, it starts out as a sexually transmitted disease. If you want to have sex with pretty girls or pretty boys then you need to at least convince yourself you're successful in some way. This builds confidence and libido, which leads to more sexual encounters, which in turn increases the desire for more sexual encounters, so you need more success.

It's a sickness, doctors don't diagnose it, psychotherapists deny it, and your children and lovers and friends and colleagues won't understand what it is you inflicted them with. And it's like AIDS – i.e. two people with AIDS still can't have sex with each other. It only makes the AIDS in both of them worse. Everyone dies faster.

HERE ARE SYMPTOMS OF THE DISEASE. And these symptoms are unavoidable. Everyone I know who has been afflicted with success has felt these and might still be feeling these:

MENTAL AND/OR PHYSICAL PAIN. Along the path to success one will inevitably encounter much failure. Pete Sampras doesn't win every tennis game. There's much loss and suffering. Some of the suffering is headaches, lack of focus (you can only focus on the objects of your success but it's hard to focus on other things that might be just as important – like taking out the garbage, or taking a walk by the river).

Physical pain is obvious. If you are building a business, for example, you won't sleep. And your body begins to break down. You gain weight. Your stomach hurts. I know executives climbing up the corporate ladder who gain weight every time politics rears it's ugly head. And politics is an inevitability of all corporate success. You need to backstab or be backstabbed. That backstabbing is real. If it's not a physical knife, it's a mental knife. Either way it destroys your body. There's so many ways pain is caused by success. What if you are sued? What if people are jealous of you and attack you in some way (could be mental, not necessarily physical). Can anyone who is successful tell me they haven't felt extreme mental and/or physical pain at some point?

SADNESS. You're not always going to win. Sometimes the pretty girl will dump you. Sometimes you lose the chess tournament. Sometimes the business fails. Sometimes the investment was a scam. Sometimes you get fired or your job is made so miserable that you are forced to quit. Then you're sad. You failed. Now you're sad. You're dejected. You're down and out. Now you look around and you realize you're on the floor and nobody wants to extend a hand to pick you up and once again, you're going to have to start all over again and make it happen and you know how hard it was that first time, second time, third time, and now here we are, the eighth time, and you have to do it again. Bullshit. That's sadness.

Anxiety. Where is she tonight? How am I going to make payroll? Or, I got the message from my boss on a Friday afternoon and I have to wait all weekend to find out the *"something serious I have to tell you"*. Or, *"will they buy my company, invest in my company, buy my product?"* Anxiety is a terrible, terrible side-effect of the success illness. Before I ever attempted any degree of success I had no anxiety. I didn't care. What a blessing that was. Unfortunately it only lasts for a few minutes. Because Success is also part of the American religion. You have to have it. Or else you can't have sex with anyone. You won't have kids. You won't have money. You won't be able to watch movies whenever you want. So the anxiety hit's again. My stomach still hurts from all the anxiety racked up from years of striving for success that was pockmarked with shingles of failure.

IGNORANCE. On the path to success it's easy to become ignorant or delusional. There's four ways you can become ignorant:

THINKING THAT SUCCESS LASTS FOREVER. For example thinking that money implies some immortality. And it might be true. Steve Jobs might be immortal.

CUTTING ETHICAL CORNERS. It's ok to tell a little white lie when over-promising and under-delivering. Or if you really need that corner office, doing a little backstabbing. Or being so afraid of being fired that someone else needs to be thrown under the truck. Just this once. Or trashing the ex of the girl when she still might have lingering feelings for him. You know it's a little bad. But everyone does it. That's success.

THINKING THAT "IF I JUST GET THIS, THEN I'LL BE HAPPY". I grew up that way. Every month, my dad had a deal that was going to close "next month." Then everything was going to be good. Then all would be well again. If I just got the girl. If she just tells me "I love you." If I just sell this company. If this one investment closes. If this one hedge fund returns 3% this month. If I can just get the "VP" title instead of the "Director" title. The "IF X, THEN HAPPY" affliction is a symptom of the success disease. I know for myself, whenever I get "X", then I want "Y". You get Money, Now Sex. You get Sex, now Love. You get Love, but you lost Money, now I need Money again. And now I need more Money. The stakes get higher. Success is a terminal disease and it only gets worse. And so on. I don't want to be on a roller coaster anymore. I want to get off the ride and go home.

FORGETTING WHO YOU ARE. You become friends with the people who will bring you closer to success. You become boring. You go to the parties and make chit-chat with the people who will bring you closer to the dream. You pretend to like the right people. You fake hating the wrong people. You eventually forget who you hate and who you like. Weren't they always hateful? It's a distant memory. You're now in the mental ward of people afflicted with the disease. You start high-fiving people you hate. You forget what you used to like. What used to give you the most substance and freedom. You smile because you read a study that people like smiling people. You shake hands firmly. You spend hours listening to people sell you something because that's part of the dance also. To be a success you need to at least pay homage to the adventures in success and excess of others.

I dated someone once who would cry at the end of every night. She had been married to someone who was fabulously wealthy and then she was divorced from him. *"You're never going to be able to take me out on that yacht in the Mediterranean,"* she would say to me. She'd be curled in the fetal position, my mattress the only piece of furniture in my apartment so we'd both be lying on it.

"That sounds so boring to me, though," I said, *"why would you even want that?"*

And she would cry more. Pull back the camera. We were in a room on 15 Broad Street, right across from the New York Stock Exchange. Pull back some more. New York City, big city of dreams. Pull back more. The frontier. The pursuit of happiness. Pull back more. We destroyed the Neanderthals. They didn't stand a chance. Success!

One more time, pull back. I was about five years old. I was with my dad. We had one of those rockets that are fueled by water. Everyone in the neighborhood gathered around. *"Stand back,"* my dad (RIP) said. And the rocket took off. It must've gone one hundred feet in the air. Everyone couldn't believe that it had actually worked. For a moment, we all tasted success. The feeling that something we cre- ated was flying through the air and maybe it would keep on going into outer space.

It was success and although it only lasted a few seconds, we never forgot how good it felt.

PART II
NOW I SEE

What is True Happiness and Success?

How to Get It, What Steps Need to be Taken to Have Success Thrown at You

Obviously we want success. And we want money. And we want all the rewards that success and money supposedly bring to us: Freedom, some degree of comfort (perhaps even luxury), some degree of protection for our descendants because we love them.

Freedom also allows us to pursue creative and/or spiritual pursuits. This ultimately is more important in life then finishing off 45 years in an office. Doesn't matter if you don't want to reach nirvana. Nirvana might not want to reach you either. But everyone wants time to sit a little. Time to think.

But we want to avoid the negative excesses of success. We want success on our terms. Not the terms of the zombies and robots that inhabit the world. We want to live, we want to be human, we want to learn how happiness, built up in a solid foundation from the inside, can bring us the success and money and love, and perhaps spiritual happiness that we deserve.

I'm going to deal a lot more with issues of success in this next section. I'm not avoiding success. In fact, I want it very much. I want money. I deserve it. And I will do good things with it. I'm convinced money belongs to me more than it belongs to just about anyone.

But a car can't ride unless everything in it is all working smoothly. Plumbing in your house won't work until all the crap is cleaned out of the pipes. A body won't survive if it's sick.

The Daily Practice

I wrote about this on my blog and in my last book.

HOWEVER, AN IMPORTANT NEW POINT:

Not everyone can do this the same way. But using the guidelines below one can build up a core practice which achieves the same goals, regardless of your life situation. If you are raising a house of five kids you are going to have some difficulties doing this. If you are 90 years old you are going to have some difficulties doing this.

My ONLY Three Goals in Life

1. I want to be happy.

2. I want to eradicate unhappiness in my life.

3. I want every day to be as smooth as possible. No hassles.

That's it. I'm not asking for much. I need simple goals else I can't achieve them.

There's been at least ten times in my life that everything seemed so low I felt like I would never achieve the above three things and the world would be better off without me. Other times I felt like I was stuck at a crossroads and would never figure out which road to take. Each time I bounced back.

When I look back at these times now I realize there was a common thread. EACH TIME THERE WERE FOUR THINGS, AND ONLY FOUR THINGS, THAT WERE ALWAYS IN PLACE IN ORDER FOR ME TO BOUNCE BACK. Now I try to incorporate these four things into a Daily Practice so I never dip low again.

The key is: every day try to make some improvement in the following areas:

PHYSICAL, EMOTIONAL, MENTAL, SPIRITUAL.

We can all agree that if we are sick, it's harder to be happy.

We can all agree that if we are in emotionally abusive relationships, it's harder to be happy.

If we are experiencing mental laziness or spiritual emptiness, it will be harder to be happy.

So each day do some of the below (or more). Over time, these exercises compound, and similar results as I describe will develop. What's different below from my prior writing on this is the modifications.

PHYSICAL – being in shape. Doing some form of exercise. In 2003 I woke up at 5am every day and from 5-6am I played "Round the World" on a basketball court overlooking the Hudson River. Every day (except when it rained). Trains would pass and people at 5:30am would wave to me out the window. Now, I try to do yoga every day. But it's hard. All you need to do, minimally, is exercise enough to break a sweat for 10 minutes. So about 20-30 minutes worth of exercise a day. This is not to get "ripped" or "shredded." But just to be healthy. You can't be happy if you aren't healthy. Also, spending this time helps your mind better deal with it's daily anxieties. If you can breathe easy when your body is in pain then it's easier to breathe during difficult situations. Here are other things that are a part of this but a little bit harder:

- Wake up by 4-5am every day.

- Go to sleep by 8:30-9. (Good to sleep 8 hours a night!)

- No eating after 5:30pm. Can't be happy if indigested at night.

MODIFICATIONS: It's easy to start off avoiding snacking in the middle of the day. Also, cut down drinking. If possible, don't drink at all. But at least cut down to half, then half again. Cut down smoking if you are a smoker. If you only sleep 5 hours a day, ask what it is you are doing that is preventing you from sleeping? Maybe but down on TV. Or, I am ashamed to say, cut down on reading. But you need 7-8 hours for a healthy mind and a healthy life.

In terms of exercise, here is the most important thing. You don't want to be 85 years old and constantly sick. You want to have high quality of life until you die. Making sure your bones are fine, making sure your spine is straight, making sure your digesting is going well, making sure you get enough sleep, these are all important things.

The most important thing is digestion. Eat foods easy to digest. Make sure you are flowing. Second most important thing: exercise. Most people can exercise 10 minutes a day. But even if you are lazy for that: try 100 pushups a day. Spread them out. 20 pushups 5 times a day. This should take up no more than eight minutes of your day and will give you the exercise you need.

Also important: stretching. You don't need to touch your toes. You just need to try to. Waiting for the bus? Try to touch your toes. While you are trying, take deep breaths. This cleans out the toxins in your body. Want to go further. Take a yoga class. Don't have time for that, try basic Ashtanga yoga moves which can be done in the privacy of your home. Check out Claudiayoga.com for the basics.

Note: this is not an infomercial. There's so much garbage out there. I don't judge the late-night infomercial people. They are just trying to make a living also. But it reminds me of one day when I was at a café and I saw a guy mixing some raw juice with an enormous amount of pink powder he was spooning out of a box where the side of the box promised "Amazing Sexual Vitality." All of that stuff is garbage. You just want to be healthy. The healthier the better (and, by the way, will lead to sexual vitality as a side effect). But the most important side effect of being healthy is that sickness will not get in the way of your freedom. It won't get in the way of mental vitality, emotional health, and ultimately spiritual health. And will allow you to enjoy high quality of life in your later years.

So find even the 10 minute routine that resonates with you. Don't depend on the late night infomercials with their false dreams and promises. The cemetery of dead exercise machines in basements is an enormous graveyard.

Emotional – If someone is a drag on me, I cut them out. If someone lifts me up, I bring them closer. Nobody is sacred here. When the plane is going down, put the oxygen mask on your face first. Family, friends, people I love – I always try to be there for them and help. But I don't get close to anyone bringing me down. This rule can't be broken. Energy leaks out of you if someone is draining you. And I never owe anyone an explanation. Explaining is draining.

Another important rule: always be honest. It's fun. Nobody is honest anymore and people are afraid of it. Try being honest for a day (without being hurtful). It's amazing where the boundaries are of how honest one can be. It's much bigger than I thought. A corollary of this is: I never do anything I don't want to do. Like, for example, I NEVER go to weddings.

When I first wrote this a lot of people commented: *"He's selfish. He'll ignore someone who needs his help."*

This is not true. If anything, I hurt someone if I try to help them when I, myself, am not healthy. I have several chapters below on how to deal with what I call "crappy people." I also have a chapter on how to deal with fear.

I'm honest. This is not a self-help book written by some perfect human being who has figured it all out. I wake up every day feeling fear and anger. These are the first exercises I have to put to work every day. See chapters below.

Someone asked me on Twitter: *"What do you see as comical in the self-help industry"?* There are several answers:

The sheer number of books from "lifestyle experts" and self-help gurus. The bottom line is: many of these people want to make money from "coaching" or seminars or motivational speaking. Power to them. Everyone needs to make a living and there's clearly an audience. But be careful because you can also die from the wrong medicine.

Many self-help gurus might be legit and are speaking from a deep, spiritual connection. Nevertheless, they've never been fired from a job, gone bankrupt, gotten divorced, have to raise kids, deal with an addiction. Or any of the above. I'm not saying I'm a self-help guy. I'm just writing from my experience. And I've dealt with ALL of the above. So take from it what you will. It's mostly my experiences I'm sharing rather than any specific advice. So when I say, "wake up at 5:30am and play basketball," it's because I did it. When I say, write down a list of ideas, it's because I was on the ground dead broke, doing nothing, crying every day, and trying to figure out how to support my family. And through diligent application of these practices (once I used medication to get out of the darkest parts of my depression) I was able to change my life around completely and come back from the land of the dead.

Many of the so-called self-help people have dealt with real world situations. I don't want to stereotype. But I would say the vast majority have not and are just trying to make a quick dollar. Like any investment, do your due diligence.

MENTAL – Every day I write down ideas. I write down so many ideas that it hurts my head to come up with one more. Then I try to write down five more. The other day I tried to write 100 alternatives kids can do other than go to college. I wrote down eight, which I wrote about here. I couldn't come up with anymore. Then the next day I came up with another 40. It definitely stretched my head. No ideas today? Memorize all the legal 2 letter words for Scrabble. Translate the Tao Te Ching into Spanish. Need ideas for lists of ideas? Come up with 30 separate chapters for an "autobiography." Try to think of 10 businesses you can start from home (and be realistic how you can execute them)? Give me 10 ideas of directions this blog can go in. Think of 20 ways Obama can improve the country. List every productive thing you did yesterday (this improves memory also and gives you ideas for today).

The "idea muscle" atrophies within days if you don't use it. Just like walking. If you don't use your legs for a week, they atrophy. You need to exercise the idea muscle. It takes about 3-6 months to build up once it atrophies. Trust me on this.

MODIFICATIONS: because the idea muscle atrophies you might not be ready to just spew ideas. Below I have a chapter on Nine Ways to Light Your Creativity on Fire. Read it.

SPIRITUAL – I feel that most people don't like the word "spiritual." They think it means "god." Or "religion." But it doesn't. I don't know what it means actually. But I feel like I have a spiritual practice when I do one of the following:

PRAY. It doesn't matter if I'm praying to a god or to dead people or to the sun or to a chair in front of me – it just means being thankful. And not taking all the credit, for just a few seconds of the day.

Or when I keep it very real, for example if I don't know what to do, I ask out loud: What is it that I am not seeing here? What do I need to understand right now? Asking is praying too, it is a way to put the question out there even if nobody is listening. Surprisingly, sometimes answers do come after asking these questions out loud. If we are willing to listen.

60 SECOND MDTN. I'm not calling it meditation. It's too hard for the average person to sit 30 minutes a day in meditation. You can meditate for 15 seconds by really visualizing what it would be like meditate for 60 minutes. The real key is to watch your thoughts not in those sixty minutes, but throughout the day labeling your thoughts. I discuss this in the chapter below, "The Power of Negative Thinking." One word on watching your thoughts: See if you can avoid judging them and just watch them, see them arising, taking shape and passing. Just watch them. If you have a hard time watching them (I do) then label them. With each thought, is it "useful" or "not useful." This is a powerful technique that gets you in control of a process in your brain which is normally automatic. Taking control of that process turns automatic into automagic.

BEING GRATEFUL. I think of everyone in my life I'm grateful for. Then I try to think of more people. Then more. It's hard, but it makes it very clear, very quickly how blessed I am to have a roof over my head, and food on the table.

FORGIVING. I picture everyone who has done me wrong. I visualize gratefulness for them (but not pity). Sometimes I cannot do it, sometimes the pain is too much, for cases like that I ask for a higher entity to be grateful for them, I delegate, fake it till I make it. Eventually with time I may be able to forgive.

STUDYING. If I read a spiritual text (doesn't matter what it is: Bible, Tao Te Ching, anything Zen related, even inspirational self-help stuff, doesn't matter) I tend to feel good. This is not as powerful as praying or meditating (it doesn't train your mind to cut out the BS) but it still makes me feel good.

My own experience: I can never achieve the three "simple" goals on a steady basis without doing the above practice on a daily basis.

And EVERY TIME I've hit bottom (or close to a bottom, or I've been at some sort of crossroads.) and started doing the above 4 items (1991, 1995, 1997, 2002, 2006, 2008) magic would happen:

The Results

- Within about one month, I'd notice coincidences start to happen. I'd start to feel lucky. People would smile at me more.

- Within three months the ideas would really start flowing, to the point where I felt overwhelming urges to execute the ideas.

- Within six months, good ideas would start flowing, I'd begin executing them, and everyone around me would help me put everything together.

- WITHIN A YEAR MY LIFE WAS ALWAYS COMPLETELY DIFFERENT. 100% upside down from the year before. More money, more luck, more health, etc. AND THEN I'D GET LAZY AND STOP DOING THE PRACTICE. And everything falls apart again. But now I'm trying to do it every day.

It's hard to do all of this every day. Nobody is perfect. I don't know if I'll do all of these things today. But I know when I do it, it works.

How to Deal With Crappy People

I'm disgusted with my brain. I see people walking down the street and there's like this killer inside me providing running nasty commentary about each person. Do you do this also?

I have to stop myself often: *"you don't know this person who is randomly crossing the street. You can't possibly know that he's a cheating lying rich Hamptons-worshipping obnoxious trust fund baby with a 17 year old mistress on the side who doesn't wipe, who doesn't wash, who would wish nothing better than to see you die."* You can't know that! So why do I think it? Most people crossing the street probably think that about me also. Who is that freak? Is he homeless? Why can't he comb his hair? Why is his fly open? Is he a child molesting pervert?

Most people are pretty crappy. But not all. And even the ones who are no good and not worthy of your time need a system for you to use so YOU can be happier and leave this lecherous gossipy crack addict thats in your head on the road and kick him or her to the curb.

THERE ARE ONLY FOUR TYPES OF PEOPLE. If you understand in advance how to deal with each of these four types you will be infinitely happier. Ultimately, interacting with the four types in the way I describe below will make one fit firmly into the first type, however difficult it is. That's the goal. You don't want to go through life unhappy.

We have just discussed the Daily Practice that has helped me out of every tough situation in my life for the past 15 years.

IT HAS 4 LEGS. Many of us focus in our daily lives on only one of the legs (Physical, Emotional, Mental, or Spiritual) but we need all the legs in balance to really sit down at the dinner table without falling.

The Practice works and brings one from the brink to success and then more success. I believe in it more than I've ever believed in any hocus-pocus anything ever.

But to develop the emotional leg of that practice takes a lot of work. It is probably the hardest. In my talks people ask about the Mental side, the idea muscle. But the Emotional side, equally as important, tends to be overlooked, dismissed even. However, it is critical.

The key is to identify the FOUR types of people and discipline yourself on how you should approach them.

The Four Types of People

#1 HAPPY. There are people who are genuinely happy in the world. Sure they have their suffering. Everyone does. But a lot of people really are pretty satisfied with their lives at this very moment.

A natural reflex (not for everyone, but certainly for some people) is to resent people for being happy. Who doesn't do that some of the time? Raise your hand!

Let's say someone lives in 20,000 square foot house in Connecticut, has a sexy wife (or sexy husband), and is genuinely happy. It's hard not to resent such a person. This resentment will block the Daily Practice from having beneficial outcomes in your life. In 2002 when I was pitching hedge fund managers to invest money with me I often ran into the exact person described above. And their families. The sexy wives in short shorts. The hedge fund managers served gourmet meals for lunchtime by loving cooks.

You can't fake resentment. You can't put on a mask. If someone is at a costume ball, you can easily see they are wearing a mask. You have to genuinely be happy for these people.

It's so hard to grab a single ounce of happiness in this world, please be happy for the ones who are happy today. Train your mind to be sincerely happy for their happiness. Catch your resentments and jealousies before they turn into monsters.

Carrie Fisher once said: *"Nobody wants to read about a good looking happy person."* She was making a commentary on comedy screenwriting and she's probably right about that. But for you to go from success to success you must first be sincerely happy for the people who are happy around you. You don't have to love them. But don't resent them.

When you truly appreciate the happiness on the outside, then you are making a nice home inside of yourself for the happiness to come inside.

#2 PEOPLE IN PAIN. I've been unhappy often. Particularly in the past decade. Sometimes things just don't work out. Sometimes people die. Sometimes parts of us die. I think the level of unhappiness and pain I've had in the past decade (versus prior decades) has taught me compassion towards others in a similar boat. Try to cultivate that compassion. It doesn't mean you have to drain yourself to help those less fortunate.

But even showing compassion and doing what you can goes a long way. If you can share what you have, all the better. If you can give a word of advice, do it. But always keep your oxygen mask handy and never hesitate to put it on you first.

Unhappy person can easily turn into category #4 below. You always have to protect yourself first. Be compassionate but keep your boundaries. Your goal is your own peace of mind throughout the day, so you can focus on your own success. The fastest way to do that is show compassion to those less fortunate. What you give, comes back tenfold. Try this exercise: picture everyone in your life who is unhappy or in pain, spend five minutes picturing them in a happier state. This trains your mind.

#3 GOOD PEOPLE. This is different from "Happy." Good people don't always have ulterior motives. Some people legitimately want to help others. There's an initial impulse (at least with me) to suspect them. To resent them. Maybe even to envy them. I envy Bill Gates being able to donate $100 billion to charity. But the best thing for me is to catch myself doing that (almost a meditation in it'self) and say, *"this guy is good. I wish I could be as good as him. I hope I can help him in any way I can."* Be grateful for all the people good to you. Five minutes a day. Doesn't have to be with incense burning and in the lotus position. On a bus, smile and think of the people you are grateful for.

And finally, the most important category of all. The category that wastes a quadrillion brain cycles a day around the world. What man can say he is Jesus and not fall prey to the ongoing anger and pain of dealing with this next category:

#4 CRAPPY PEOPLE: PEOPLE WHO WILL DO YOU HARM, no matter what you do, for no reason at all. They never will get it. They will say and do things to you and they will never ever understand how evil they are.

And you will hate them. HATE THEM. And they knock on the door of your brain at three in the morning and they want to yell at you. And you yell back. And they yell back. And on and on. All day. All afternoon. The ongoing conversation with the shittiest people in the world. They will torture you, kill you, rape your wife and slit the thoughts out of your mind and not even care because they think they are doing the right thing. YOU KNOW WHO I'M TALKING ABOUT. Because you have a good 20 or 30 of these in your life just like I do. They might even be former friends, relatives, neighbors, bureaucrats, whatever, whoever, whenever. They swoop down on your life and are just plain crappy and they won't even know it.

Sometimes, in a weak moment, I think to myself: What if I run into them again? How badly I will hurt and destroy them. Maybe just casually walk up to them and smash a glass over their head so their nose is broken, glasses broken on the floor, blood all over their face. Arm broken after I hold the elbow and stomp on it.

STOP!

Similarly, I was talking to someone the other day who couldn't stop talking about someone who had wronged her fourteen years ago. Stop! You are an idiot. And it's boring already. It was your fault anyway! Meaning: if you are still angry about an event from 14 years ago then it no longer has to do with the person who wronged you, its now all about you. The past is long gone, historical is hysterical, and the events are now just lingering inside of you. Say goodbye to them. Now.

This is the worst category. I'll tell you one more anecdote. One time someone posted a horrible comment on my blog. I won't repeat it. Racist, mean, rude to me, whatever. I deleted the post, blocked the user, blocked his IP address. And then I was going to send him an email telling him what I thought of him. I was angry. Then I stopped myself. YOU HAVE TO STOP YOURSELF.

Remember this:

WHEN YOU GET IN THE MUD WITH A PIG, YOU GET DIRTY AND THE PIG GETS HAPPY.

There is only ONE only way to deal with these people in a way that will make you happier instead of sadder. ONE WAY. And it always works. This is the most important part of the Emotional leg of the Daily Practice. COMPLETELY IGNORE THE EVIL PEOPLE:

- COMPLETELY IGNORE THEM.

- DON'T THINK ABOUT THEM.

- DON'T TALK TO THEM.

- DON'T WRITE THEM.

- MOST IMPORTANT: DON'T GIVE THEM ADVICE. They will NEVER listen to your advice. It's arrogant and stupid to think they will. It will only lead to more cycles of pain for you. The goal for me is to stop all cycles that cause me any pain at all. Giving advice to crappy people will only result in more pain for you. That's the only possible result. Much better to be happy than to flush knotted up brown advice down a toilet that caused you agony to push out. This is hard.

- MOST IMPORTANT: NEVER GOSSIP ABOUT THEM behind their backs. Just completely disregard. We don't care about their happiness or how evil they are. We only care about you. It's. Never ever talk about them behind their backs. Repeat this 500 times. And if this is difficult, it's because is an addiction.

This is a daily discipline. Much easier to do a 1000 pushups. I had an article recently on the Wall St Journal site that had 971 comments. No exaggeration when I say 950 of the smartest anonymous trolls on the internet called me an idiot moron and worse. I ignored all the comments. Great. I could care less. I was the winner there.

Then I put another article up on a supposedly peaceful site about Buddhism and yoga, the Elephant Journal. Very inspiring site and I post there regularly. The topic of my post was that 18 year olds should basically not be sent into war. I like peace. Better to send 40 year olds. They are closer to death anyway. The most hateful responses popped up. People were comparing me to Hitler. I was so shocked I wasted one whole night until 2 in the morning responding to these people but ignoring the many emails I get that genuinely support me and that I want to be friends with.

WHY DID I DO THAT? I wanted my haters to like me. I wanted them to agree with me and love me. It's like putting a gun to your head and saying, *"unless you do what I say, I will kill myself."* You're going to end up firing that gun.

I lost my discipline for a whole night and then I slept late and it took at least 36 hours to get back on track. What a waste. For nothing! It may be hard to keep up this practice. BUT YOU FAIL AND DIE UNHAPPY IF YOU DON'T.

And did I win a trophy for doing this? Was it a huge trophy made of gold for responding to all of those comments? Did everyone/anyone write back and say: "You're right. I'm sorry. Now I LOVE you! Let's all be lovers!" Of course not! They just want to fight. I got in the mud with pigs. I GOT DIRTY.

If someone says, *"what do you think of so-and-so,"* your worst enemy, you say back, "SO-AND-SO WHO?" And that's it. No explanation. Nothing more. "So and so who?" Then change subject right away.

This is the emotional leg of the Daily Practice and must be balanced with the other three legs. Any deviation will set you back. Any addiction to the opposite of the above behaviors will eat you alive like cockroaches feasting on your heart. Have a good night.

A LOT OF PEOPLE HAD ADDITIONAL QUESTIONS ABOUT MY ARTICLE: "How to Deal with Crappy People". HERE ARE MY RESPONSES.

Q: SERIOUSLY? YOU WALK AROUND THINKING STUFF LIKE THAT ABOUT TOTAL STRANGERS, WHO HAVE NEVER SO MUCH AS LOOKED AT YOU, LET ALONE HARMED YOU?

A: Yes. Seriously. Maybe you are judging me?

My challenge is to either own that dialogue or I risk having it owning me. The only way to make my thoughts my slaves is to notice them, watch them in action, and transform them.

Q: MY OWN PARENTS HAVE EVIL TENDENCIES, BUT I DON'T THINK THEY TRULY REALIZE IT. HOW THEN, DO YOU IGNORE THESE PEOPLE, ESPECIALLY WHEN THEY ARE AROUND OTHER PEOPLE YOU WANT TO SEE AND INTERACT WITH?

A: This is the crux of the whole article. In fact, it's usually the people closest to you that affect you the most! After all they have years of experience knowing who you were (before you started getting real while reading this book), they know what buttons to press, and it is difficult It's to ignore them.

Do this:

NEVER GOSSIP ABOUT THEM behind their backs. You already can't stand being around them. Why keep them with you in your thoughts when they are no longer there. NEVER, ever gossip.

When they are around, DON'T "ENGAGE." If someone wants to pick a fight, let them pick a fight with the air. Say: *"Well, I have to go now"* and if you can leave, leave. Or go into another room for a while. Or change the topic if it's at a dinner table. Don't play with the pigs.

I don't mean being passive aggressive by changing the topic, that could back-fire. In such a case you want to state your needs clearly. You could say: *"You know [name]? thinking/talking about this upsets me, could we talk about something else?"* That way you acknowledge the person, state your needs, and clarify what you will and will not tolerate. Then if your wish is not respected, walking away from the table is not passive aggressiveness, it is keeping it real. Walk away and do not look back. Leave if you have to. Tend to your soul. Put your own mask first.

This trains them to treat you better. If they want a response from you at all, they begin to learn what gets that response. Else they don't get to interact with you. Period.

VERY IMPORTANT TO REMEMBER THESE TWO THINGS:

1. You can't win the fight.

2. You can't give advice (i.e. nothing you say will make their lives better or convince them you are right about something).

Turn down as many invitations as possible to get together. You need to take a break from this person. "HISTORICAL IS HYSTERICAL." Just focus on your own present, the family and friends who love you and need you, your responsibilities, and engage as little as possible with the people who abuse you or bring up the past or demand an apology, or whatever. You need a break. And they need to be trained.

Q: What if it's a co-worker.

A: Remember these things:

- Never gossip behind their back.

- No small talk! No flirting. Ever. Just don't engage beyond what the work requires.

- Always give them credit for work they did.

- Don't worry about always having your opinions heard and agreed with.

- If it's ruining your work environment to the point where you can't stand it, look for another job.

- Be fully professional. Don't get emotional. Document every meeting, email, and interaction. Give them a copy of the documentation saying "This is what I understand...," etc. When you are fully professional, it trains the people around you, crappy or otherwise.

- I'll repeat: Never gossip behind their back or say anything bad about them. If you clean the shit in front of your own door then there's a decent chance they will clean theirs. This is the most important rule when dealing with a crappy co-worker.

- By the way, things don't get cured in 24 hours, especially in the workplace. Give it time. But follow these rules and keep it clean. No slipping! You're a dead man if you do.

- And if it is really that bad, look for another job.

Q: What if it's a family member and I feel guilty ignoring them or not calling them or returning their calls/invitations?

A: The key in your question is *"I feel guilty."* You need to work with your guilt. At this point it has nothing to do with them, else you can use my answer above regarding parents/family members. Ask yourself, *"what do you feel guilty about?"*, *"what is the worst that can happen?"*, *"are you afraid these people won't love you anymore?"*, *"what would the consequences of that be?"* *"Is there a middle ground?"*

When you feel uncomfortable about a situation (and "guilt" is certainly uncomfortable) it's a valuable opportunity for self-enquiry. Ask as many questions as possible so you can get to know who this creature is, this discomfort, that is actually LIVING inside of you. Guilt is a form of blindness. Now we want to See.

IF YOU ABSOLUTELY FEEL THAT IT'S IMPORTANT TO REPAIR RELATIONS THEN DO THIS: WRITE THEM A LETTER. In the letter say:

- Thank you for your invitations (or calls).

- What you miss about them. Why you love them. Keep it VERY-brief.

- Give the rules for future interactions: list what you would like to have happen so you don't feel abused or hurt. DON'T DEMAND AN APOLOGY. Historical is hysterical.

You have been kind, you clearly expressed how certain behaviors made you feel, you educated them on what you can and cannot tolerate in order to keep your spirit healthy, and you did all of it with grace and compassion. If the rules can't be followed, then that's it. No interactions and nothing for you to feel guilty about.

Q: SHOULD I LOOK AT "CRAPPY PEOPLE" WITH COMPASSION?

A: Several people in the comments suggested this. IF SOMEONE IS CRAPPY TO YOU, THEY ARE NOT WORTH YOUR COMPASSION. We have to keep it real. If someone has just slandered you to someone else, or if an ex is trying to prevent you from seeing your kids, or if you just caught your boyfriend with another girl in bed, or if a friend borrowed money and refuses to return it, etc. then it's not reality that you're going to be compassionate with them the next minute. Forget it!

It's like exercise. If you lift too much weight for your body to handle then you hurt yourself. Sometimes very badly. Same thing here. If you try to find compassion for horrible people then you might severely damage your happiness prospects. FAKE COMPASSION LEADS TO DELUSION! Try first: NON-HATE. If someone does something hateful, tell them it's hateful, but then practice non-hate. Walk away. Ignore them. Stop listening to them and move away. Non-hate is a powerful skill. I leave compassion (in this particular case) for Buddhas. I'm not one of them. Chances are neither are you, at least not yet.

How do you practice non-hate? With crappy people assume that:

- They have their problems also.

- Maybe they weren't loved enough as children or whatever.

- They chose to take out some of their anger on me. They didn't think it through.

- I clearly don't love them but I'm going to choose not to hate them.

And then that's it. I move on. I stop thinking of them. I don't talk to them. I don't talk about them. I don't love them. I don't hate them. They don't exist.

I was talking to a friend of mine who had been best friends for years with someone named Bill (name made up). Bill had then stolen from him. I asked him about Bill recently and what was going on. He turned to me and, as sincerely as possible so I really felt he meant it: he said, "BILL WHO?" and that's the attitude you should take.

COMPASSION IS TOO HARD. DON'T TOUCH YOUR TOES ON THE FIRST DAY YOU'VE EVER STRETCHED IF YOUR BODY IS NOT FLEXIBLE.

Don't try to be Buddha. Compassion can actually hurt you. Practice Non-Hate first.

Q: HOW DO YOU DEAL WITH CRAPPY PEOPLE YOU CAN'T IGNORE BECAUSE YOU WANT TO ENJOY THE NON CRAPPY PEOPLE THEY MIGHT BE RELATED TO/MARRIED TO, ETC.?

A: Same as the "family" one above. You have to see them. You have to be around them. But just don't engage. Don't get into an argument even when they provoke. Say "hello" and "goodbye" and even a pleasant response if they ask a pleasant question. Train them on how they need to treat you. Try not to be passive aggressive either. Just practice non-hate.

But, the primary advice still holds: ignore them, don't engage with them, don't respond when provoked, leave when provoked, don't talk about them afterwards. TRAIN THEM. But also train yourself not to get in the mud with a pig, even in your mind when they are nowhere to be seen. What a waste of brain cycles then.

Q: WHAT IF THE CRAPPY PERSON IS YOUR BOSS?

Work hard, don't engage when they try to bait you, be incredibly professional, document all meetings and interactions and give them a copy, give them credit, no flirting, no gossiping, don't talk about them behind their back.

Q: WHEN IS REVENGE JUSTIFIED?

A: NEVER. It is never ever justified. I have had people do horrible things to me. Horrible. But let's say I have 40 years left to live on this life. Any time spent on revenge will reduce the number of happy days I have left. Not only is revenge never warranted but even thinking about it wastes brain cycles.

It's like in the above example: "BILL WHO?" That's why it's such a great saying, "the best revenge is living well." I have plenty of ways to revenge the stupid, crappy people I've had to deal with. I'd rather walk by the Hudson River, read a book, and have a waffle. (Note: if we are talking about violence, there are proper channels for dealing with it: police, support groups, documentation, etc.)

Q: I THINK THERE IS YET ANOTHER GROUP OF PEOPLE – THE STUPID PEOPLE. THEY MAY ALSO DO YOU HARM, BUT ONLY BECAUSE OF SHEER STUPIDITY. WHAT DO YOU THINK?

A: Same thing. If someone abuses you, regardless of their IQ, they are still crappy people. Stupid people who are abusive equals crappy people.

It doesn't matter their IQ. You can't waste time being abused or dealing with people who don't treat you right. You can't train them to be smarter, but you can train them not to abuse you. Or there will be no interaction.

Q: It seems you have been inspired by a negative comment you got. It sounds like you aren't following your own rules?

A: This was actually inspired by a 2500 year old book I was reading. But yeah, I'm in the same club everyone else is. We all have crappy people to deal with. These are the best approaches for dealing with these.

Nobody here is trying to be a Buddha. It's too hard! Buddha spent years trying to be Buddha. Gandhi spent years trying to be Gandhi. I get annoyed and pissed off every day.

I will say this: I have a lot of experience following this advice and I have a lot of experience not following it.

When I follow it, my life is a lot better. I'm happier, and ultimately the crappy people around me either disappear or they start interacting with me in a better way.

When I don't follow it: my time spent arguing with these people gets greater. My time spent talking about them gets greater. My time spent thinking about these people increases. So even if I might have had just a five minute argument with them, suddenly it takes away maybe 50 hours of my life. That's an ugly way to live.

So it's simple: better for me to follow my own advice than to not follow it. I can't lift 200 lbs the first day I ever go to the gym but I can work on it, be aware of the importance of practice, and work on improving every day.

Q: What if you are the crappy person?

A: This is a great question. It almost sounds like it was intended as a joke but it's actually an important point. Many of us are the crappy people and we don't realize it. But the point is how to DEAL WITH what I define as the four types of people.

If you are real enough to notice you are a crappy person then you, my friend, have taken a huge step. You're already less of a crappy person because you're being honest with yourself. You've become less delusional.

Following the suggestions in the original article and you quickly move from mostly being a #4 to becoming a #1.

Your energy will be redirected, it will be more efficient, you will become less of a crappy person. Guaranteed. It's a practice. Nobody gets to be Buddha in 24 hours.

This is all part of the "Emotional" leg of what I describe as "The Daily Practice" in another post. Each leg is important. 4 legs to a chair so you can sit.

Q: IF A CRAPPY PERSON PHYSICALLY TOUCHES YOU, YOU CAN'T IGNORE THAT. YOU'VE GOT TO GET VIOLENT AND FEEL GOOD ABOUT IT. RIGHT?

A: RUN!!! If you can run, run. If you need police, get police. If you need help, get help.

VERY IMPORTANT: FEELING GOOD ABOUT HURTING SOMEONE CAN GET YOU KILLED AND IS A HORRIBLE LEAK OF YOUR ENERGY.

If someone is attacking you, then defend to the point where you can run away as quickly as possible. If someone attacks someone right next to you, then help that person to run away or, if they are staying and fighting, then you run away and get help.

A few years ago a friend of mine got in a fight at a bar. I wasn't there. My friend is a good guy. But he decided he couldn't let someone be abusive to him so he made the decision to fight back. He got hit on the head. Now my friend is paralyzed from the neck down for the rest of his life. 25 years old. The best thing you can do is run or find help.

Q: Was this post about me?

Five people asked me this question. The answer is no. It's not about "you" or anyone I know.

Conclusion:

There's one theme: you want to be a happy person. You don't want to be a crappy person. Forget everyone else for a second. Forget the people who are abusing you or who have been abusive to you. Your goal is to use these techniques to as quickly as possible, become a consistently happy person. That's more important than winning a fight. It's more important than gossiping or feeling guilty. It's not about being right, it's about being HAPPY.

Am I a happy person? Not always. Sometimes I'm a pretty crappy person. But I'm hoping my ratio of happy over crappy is getting better.

The Power of Negative Thinking

One person in the comments of one of my articles posted an exercise of what to do about these people. WARNING LABEL: THE EXERCISE THIS PERSON SUGGESTED WILL DESTROY YOU IF YOU TRY IT.

(If you try to be the Dalai Lama you might disappoint yourself and die.)

I think it's very damaging what this person suggested. In the exercise she suggested you imagine a world filled with love. You think of the people you love, and then you picture the people you hate and you imagine you have the same sort of love towards them.

This will break your brain in two. It will break your soul into pieces. Unless I suddenly turn into Jesus or Buddha I'm not going to love these people. Picture the person you hate most. Can you really suddenly turn that hate into love via mental visualization. That's more like mental masturbation.

In a blog post I wrote about plugging your leaks I mentioned three intensities of leaks: mild, moderate, intense. It's the same here. You might be angry at someone in a mild way, a moderate way, or in a very intense way.

All are equally bad. BUT THERE'S NO WAY YOU CAN GO FROM "INTENSE" HATRED TO COMPASSIONATE UNCONDITIONAL LOVE. Gratuitous positive thinking for the sake of being positive just doesn't work. There are many deep, reasons, dating from childhood that you don't even understand that might cause you to have intense hatred or anger. Trying to skip all of that so you can feel a fake love will only turn you into a fake and create even more of a monster.

There's simply no reason to feel compassion towards anyone other than the people who you are closest to.

So here's what you do. It's a mental discipline. If you can do this, it not only deals with these people it will change your life so much you'll feel like you suddenly generated super powers. Your productivity goes up. Your capability of dealing with pain and suffering goes up tenfold, and your ability to problem-solve turns you into a miracle man. You also might start to be aware of issues you never knew you had.

In other words, you'll get luckier when everyone else is floundering around lost in their pathetic thoughts of murder and mayhem. You become human in a zoo filled with animals. I'm not kidding. You WILL become a superhero.

How to cultivate Non-Hate

Everytime you are thinking about someone on your list, try to catch yourself. This is the hard part. Stop yourself for just a second in the middle of your mental maze of anguish. Label the thought you were thinking "useful" or "not useful." If someone shat on my face and now I'm thinking about my mental argument with him or her. This is "not useful." If you label enough thoughts "not useful" then

"Intense" anger might turn into "Moderate" anger. "Moderate" anger might turn into "Mild" anger. This is how you cultivate non-hate instead of compassion. It works. I do it. I can tell you it works.

You might still have to deal with this person (at work, for instance) but your entire dynamic with the person will begin to change and you will see results. They will feel the dynamic. The world will feel it. Everything will change. Not overnight but over time. Intensity on this major leak of your energy goes down. And this is a MAJOR leak.

THE HARDEST PART is stopping yourself long enough to do the labeling. The "not useful." But if you can do that you'll find this technique also comes in handy in other parts of life.

Like where you feel GREED or envy towards someone ("not useful") or where you feel delusional (daydreaming about what you'd do with the billion dollars you're going to make on the sewing machine you're going to invent – "Not useful"). This also goes for when you are talking to someone else about the person who makes you upset (angry gossip is "not useful") or when something bad happens to the person and you think that's just fine ("approval" of bad things is "not useful").

Most things in life, in fact, aren't very useful to think about ("The IMF," "Greece," "most politics," "family I don't like," "ex-friends/girlfriends," etc.)

What's the outcome of all of this if you get good at this labeling? It's as if you've been in a horrible accident that ruins the body you spent a lifetime creating. Suddenly you've been rebuilt. Everything that was ugly and hideous sheds away. You become beautiful.

Fight Fear

I'm tired of being afraid. From the moment we're born we are always in a fight. We fight to eat, we fight to stand up, we fight to control our bowels. Finally we shit by ourselves, in clean porcelain bowls. What an achievement! The first of many. The first of many happinesses that become aborted, miscarried joy strewn everywhere throughout our lives as we hurry to our death.

We fight to have friends. We fight the bullies. We fight the girls who think we're too disgusting to touch. We're afraid to be unloved, unwanted, unworthy.

"It's better not to touch him," Karen N said to her friends at square dance class in 7th grade. They would hold their hands out, grasping the air in front of me, while we dosi-doed and pretended to love each other.

We graduate to the real world. So now we can fight bosses, employees, colleagues, competitors. Each one of our thoughts costumed into spoken words we think will bring us more money, more happiness. Those same oaths of loyalty, of hope and fearlessness all vomited back in our faces.

"You're disgusting," said one close relative who took too close a look at my face when I was 16. I wish I could google all of the conversations of my life for the phrase *"you're disgusting."* Catalog them and browse them in my old age.

And then we're afraid. Because these fights cost time and/or money. So we fight for money. And sometimes we kill for it or go to jail for it or lie for it or steal for it. But always we're afraid of it.

I'm tired of fighting. Kids, parents, siblings, people I work with, others others OTHERS. I look at them through a kaleidoscope. One time they are a beautiful image all mixed together, but then I shift ever so slightly and everything becomes dissonant, a collage of colors that never should've been put together.

I'm tired of the non-stop battle. Where we always want things we can't afford. People we can't have. Situations that eluded us. Situations that deluded us.

I'm tired of it.

It's time to open the eyes. Time to see.

In 2002 I'd walk with my business partner, Dan, in between trades. The market was going down every day. We'd daytrade the worst stocks, buying companies that were down 30% in a day. These were always the stocks sure to bounce. The stocks that the girls wouldn't touch at the dance. The companies nobody loved.

We'd walk on streets like Rutgers St, or Henry St. Streets that were off the standard NYC grid. Streets with weird temples to no religion and tiny slivers of a hole in the wall that you'd stick a dollar through and a dirty hand would hand you back a dumpling. *"I could live here,"* I said. *"And completely disappear. Nobody would know I ever existed."*

But of course I can't. I'd bring my wife now. My two kids. I'd have to worry about my bank account. I have people who depend on me. I'd still call Dan throughout the day wondering about deals that would never happen. Chinatown is far away for me now.

If I drilled a tunnel straight through the center of the Earth and ended up on the other side it wouldn't even matter. I'd be right back where I started. Afraid of all the people around me, everyone speaking languages I never really understood in the first place.

I'm just really tired of the constant fight.

DON'T READ NEWSPAPERS. All they do is bring you more fear. My kids came over today and said, *"Did you hear about the kid in Brooklyn?"* No, I said. And I don't want to. Whether the news is true or sad or horrible or horrific, it doesn't matter to me. I don't read the newspaper. They shit fear and then try to make it smell good so they can sell it to you for $1.25. Even at the tender ages of 9 and 12 my kids are already being programmed by the media to have knee-jerk reactions to the fear they try to spread. The media doesn't care. They'll scare my kids about radiation from Japan one week, and kids being molested the next, and Swine Flu the next. Anything to tug at their heart strings that are only just beginning to be tuned. Let's make sure they are tuned to the correct key.

DON'T WATCH TV. Jealousy, greed, anger, murder are the themes of the top TV shows. And then there's the news. I have one or two shows I'll download on itunes and that's it. The rest of the cable companies could shut down for all I care.

TRY TO SLEEP 8-9 HOURS. Fear is the enemy of sleep. It's a monster that sit's on you all night trying to wake you. The less you sleep, the more that monster can whisper in your brain during the day.

PRACTICE INVISIBILITY. Nobody will miss you today if you take a break from Twitter, Facebook, Google+, Linkedin, and whatever else is out there. Your klout ranking doesn't matter. Your number of followers on twitter won't make you happier. Take a break for a day. Or two. Or limit your usage on these media to a specific time each day.

I'm not down on social media. In fact, it's become perhaps my ONLY outlet for being social on many days, other than interactions with my wife. It's just that there's ways for it to be addictive, or a negative force. It's common now for divorce lawyers to ask new clients, is your husband or wife spending a lot of time on Facebook. There's a lot of intrigue that goes into social media. It's safe, there's no touch (at first) and it can easily escalate. That's great for shy, single people. Not so great for married people.

However, being reliant on it is an addiction. Try to tone it down just a notch and read a book instead. See if it makes a difference in happiness. If not, then no worries.

On my particular Twitter feed, I follow many reporters. So, consequently, I get their latest news articles. Which are often scary and depressing. Because, by definition, they are in the media. For some people, your twitter feed might be different and more valuable as a resource, particularly if you are trying to find uplifting outlets.

NO ALCOHOL. This is hard for almost everybody, even me. Alcohol is a way of life. You go outside at night, and you drink alcohol with your friends. People often think alcohol pushes away the fear but it just "kicks the can" (I have to put it in quotes because now financial media is using that term too often to describe events on a beach resort in Europe) until the fear becomes a monster that wakes you up on a sugar bounce in the middle of the night. Plus alcohol deludes you into thinking you have no inhibitions when in fact, you never had any inhibitions. It's just that nobody else knew that.

If you really want to be hardcore about this, and I highly recommend this if you truly want to fight the fear:

- No alcohol.

- No hanging out with people who drink .

- No dinner past 5pm .

- Sleep by 8:30pm

I suggested this to a friend of mine who was constantly depressed. She cries herself to sleep every night. After a night of binge eating and drinking and socializing with people who she then complains about the next day.

But her response on my suggestion: *"I can't."*

So that's that. Some people can't. But try to at least cut down on the alcohol, which is a fatal drug and is also a depressant.

EXPRESS YOURSELF. Paint something today. Or write down the list of ideas you have. Or write a poem even if you've never read or written one in your entire life. Or write a story about your earliest memories. All the colors you saw on that memory. List the colors. List the family members who were there, list the location. Spend a half hour today expressing yourself in some way. List what you wish you had done differently the first time you felt passionate for something or someone. You can even express yourself through email. Return an email from 2004. Just pull it up right now. You never returned it. Return it right now.

IMAGINE YOU SUDDENLY HAD NO MONEY OR JOB OR LOVE AT ALL. List everything that would mean for you. You would still be able to stay in shape. Still be able to have compassion towards the people around you. Still be able to generate ideas. Still surrender to the universe around you. From there you can rebuild. I've been there and had to do it.

USEFUL/NOT USEFUL. See the above chapter on the Power of Nega-tive Thinking. This is a very powerful tool to discipline your mind. The ideal is to practice this when you aren't afraid or angry. Be-cause when you are in the throes of obsession and fear your mind needs to be a disciplined tool in order to apply this technique.

I find it to be a great technique for dealing with fear. Insomnia grays our days, cancer might be bleeding up slowly from our rec-tum to our heart, mental illness might be fogging the lenses we use see all life around us, but you can still try and train your thoughts to take out the pieces that are clouded with delusion and fear.

ASK YOURSELF THE OPPOSITE. I kick myself for all the times I've been afraid when and I spent the day pacing and anxious and wor-ried and frightened and then, guess what – the thing I was afraid of never happened. One time I had made an investment. I called the guy in charge of the investment. He didn't pick up. For the next 45 minutes I got so anxious I had assumed the guy was now in Brazil and enjoying all my money. I couldn't get the thought out of my head. I became obsessed. Then he called back (he was in a meeting, or having sex, or whatever) and he was like, *"what's up?"* and my fears were obviously for naught.

This always happens. 99% of the things we fear never happen. From 1950 – 1990 everyone was afraid the Soviet Union any day was going to drop a nuclear bomb on us. They had the bombs AND their leaders were insane, just like our leaders were. Any-thing could've happened. But nothing ever did. All the fears were flushed down the toilet.

So here's what you can do, another way to train your mind similar to the above technique. Ask yourself the opposite. For instance, I'm always afraid I'm going to make a series of decisions which will ultimately result in me going broke. Well, what if every time I have that fear I ask myself, *"What if I don't go broke?"* Which is the likely outcome (god, I hope so! Now I'm afraid again!) . Training your mind to ask the opposite at least confuses it enough you can move on with your life. Always move towards the opposites on any of these types of negative thoughts, particularly when they occur at 3 in the morning and you are feeling that nagging urge to pace.

We're so happy when we're young and the future seems infinite in front of us. But it is an engorged cyst with pus that leaks out and finally bursts when youth turns to old age, when potential turns to mediocrity, when love turns to languish.

But while we hurry to our death, and the last liquid pus comes streaming out of the cyst of our youth, when the colors of our hopes turns to the grays of insomnia, it's time to realize that none of it ever mattered – that freedom is colorless.

Obstacles to Success

I really blew it and everyone knows it. It's funny how many times now I'm even asked to speak at conferences about failure and about all the times I've failed at businesses, in love, in career, in school, in writing, in whatever it is I was attempting to do that left me on the floor of a hotel room crying, alone, drinking, whatever.

I'm like Dr. Failure. I know exactly what you need to do if you want your wife to hate you, if you want to get thrown out of school, if you want to lose your investors $100 million. If you want to lose your home, andso on.

1/16 of the time people are happy. The rest of the time they are unhappy. So if you start to avoid all the things that cause unhappiness then maybe there's a small chance you can improve the ratios in your favor

Here's the REAL reasons entrepreneurs fail. It's not because of a bad programmer. Fire him and get a new one. It's not because a client pulled out at the last minute. Get a new client, or anticipate. It not because your girlfriend cheated on you. Kick her to the curb. It's not because some guy sued you or your employees delivered an unfinished product. Every failure failure boils down to these core reasons that come from the INSIDE. Some might seem obvious but they really are the ONLY reasons for failure. They are the CORE FOUNDATIONS of every failure. Pay attention to them:

SICKNESS. This is obvious. If you are sick all the time, you won't be successful at a business. When I was a venture capitalist I would never invest money to a guy hooked up to a ventilator. Or even if I suspect they are clinically depressed. Many people avoid second dates if they find out on the first date the girl has late-stage terminal cancer. This is sad but reality.

What does it mean for an entrepreneur? Put good things in your body. Exercise. Don't drink. Sleep 8 hours a day. That's it. Then you probably won't get sick as much and you'll have a lot of energy to do your business. If you're sick in bed all the time, your business will fail.

Sometimes Sickness might also be telling you something. When I worked for a private equity firm I fell once for no reason and could barely walk for a week or so afterwards. It wasn't good for me to be there. I never went back. And later experiences proved me correct. Your body sometimes knows more than you do. Listen to it.

INERTIA. I went out for dinner the other night with people who couldn't stop talking, eating, and drinking. One person had business ideas. The other person wanted to write a novel. All night long drinking, eating, talking about business ideas, talking about writing novels. Talking, eating, drinking, talking, walking, drinking again, talking more. Then you sleep. Wake up at eight. Bloated, sick, heavy.

Wake up at eight – then you are too late. If you want to succeed you first have to get up and start. You can't watch SharkTank, you have to be the shark. Don't waste time. Start NOW. No more stuffing your face. No more parties at high-tech meetups with lots of social media experts. You know you only want to have sex with a social media expert. Stop lying about it. Start your business, blog, little shop.

DOUBTS. You need to have a real passion behind the product you are creating. Would YOU use the product? If you wouldn't, or if you are not sure, then you have doubts. Steve Jobs WANTED an ipad, an ipod, an i-everything. Doubts will make you fail because you won't be able to make critical design decisions. Decisions are the top of a pyramid. Beneath the top is the base built by your solid foundation:

"This is the product I would use. This is the product I want!" Then all decisions come from that.

With stockpickr.com I was obsessed about putting in new features. But every single new feature was something that had worked successfully to make me a better trader. I had no doubts. I had the spreadsheets showing me those strategies worked. With Reset.com I only built websites that I would want to use.

LAZINESS. Everyone is lazy some of the time. If I am bored with something I'm lazy. But with a startup, or if you are trying to move up in the corporate world, or if you are falling in love with a girl, you can't be lazy. She wants to go dancing tango. You want to watch Jay Leno. You're a lazy pig. She'll find someone else to tango with. You have to be working at it all the time, except when you sleep and exercise and even then your subconscious is working at it. For jobs and startups, it's a 10-12 hour day. There's no avoiding it. Managing that time is a different story but that's how you beat the 9 hour a day competitors.

CARELESSNESS. If your programmers present you a final product, you still have to check every page, click on everything, click on everything fast and twice, don't forget a birthday or an anniversary, remember everything your boss told you or everything the client wanted. Be detail oriented. Pay attention. Clear your mind and listen to what is actually being said.

Persistent carelessness equals consistent failure.

VACILLATING. *"Is this the right business? Or should I back up and start fresh with a new idea? Should I hire this girl? Or that guy? I'll hire this guy but then I'll have doubts and I won't follow up. I'll go out with this girl who is rich but maybe I really like that sexy girl who I met in an elevator."* If you're stuck in too many middles, you get sliced up into bits of broken glass. Your businesses implodes, your relationships have to start back at zero. You vacillated and ended up with nothing. Congratulations.

NO PROGRESS. You start your business. You launch your dating site.A few people sign up. But there's no excitement. People stop signing up. Traffic stays a few dozen people a day. Ok, no progress.

You buy some google ads. They sort of work. No progress. BY THE WAY, FAILURE IS NOT A STIGMA. IT'S OK TO FAIL. It's just that having "no progress" might be an indication you need to move to another idea or business. I have a post coming about this about another business I started where I was making no progress so I stopped the business and had to return money on the eve of raising it. I was shaking when I returned the money. I don't like to give back $500,000 that had my name on it. I was a failure. But ultimately returning the money on the eve of failure created much goodwill and led to greater success later. This is not about the success of one business or failure. THIS IS ABOUT THE SUCCESS OF YOU.

DELUSIONS. People start a business, then they think it's the best geo-locator mobile dating discount app on the universe: *"it's called '6th Circle' because it's a play on "foursquare" and the sixth circle of Dante's Inferno. We're going to do five deals with major sidewalk companies in China to get the word out. The market is $18 billion in profit's because we get everyone in Shanghai to pay 10 cents a day."* Blah blah. Always look back. *"Am I smoking crack?"* *"Am I smoking crack?"* *"Am I smoking crack?"* Every day check the ashtray. IS THERE CRACK IN THERE? Delusions will keep you from making progress. Then suddenly, no money, no friends, no more PR, and you're on your bed smoking your last piece of crack hanging onto the lonely panties of the last hooker who left you by yourself, not even bothering to dress as she slammed the door on the way out. This is your mind on crack.

YOU FALL BACKWARDS. You're losing clients. Your best programmer quit. Your traffic is going down. Your girlfriend is not returning your calls. Your boss promoted someone over you. Time to get creative now. You need to think out of the box. Again, this is just an obstacle. Not a failure. Failures start off as obstacles. You want to overcome obstacles. You can't make your girlfriend call you back. Maybe you get a new girlfriend who calls you back. Maybe you take a step back and build a new site. You start looking for a new job so you find people who value you. Falling backwards consistently will make you go to zero. So when you start to "fall backwards" you say, *"ok, I have an obstacle. Now I need to think out of the box to get rid of this obstacle."* It's not bad to have obstacles. You just have to overcome them. If you fall back too far then you fell down.

Consistently having ANY of the nine items above will make your business fail. And will make them succeed if you avoid ALL of them. I say "consistently." BE VIGILANT. EVERY MORNING REVIEW THE POTENTIAL OBSTACLES. EVERY AFTERNOON. EVERY NIGHT. Catch yourself when you first hit the obstacle. If you can clean the obstacles out, you'll have success. Guaranteed.

Follow the Daily Practice. I outline and obstacles will be easier to catch before you fail. TRUST IT. That Practice will work. It works for me. I see it work every day for others. Businesses might fail, relationships might not work out, your old boss will be stuck yelling at the dead pieces of meat that sit in his office sucking up to him. Everyone in the world is suing everyone else and blaming their old best friends. Your ex-girlfriend is busying being unhappy in her next relationship. But no longer can anything stop you from succeeding.

Do You Have to be Rich to be Honest?

I got this email a few months ago: *"you must be totally loaded to write the kind of stuff you do."*

Another person wrote me, *"I'm not rich enough to be as honest as you are. I'd lose my job and customers."*

Finally, after I got several emails like this I asked someone back, *"Why do you think I'm rich? Do you think someone needs to be wealthy in order to be honest?"*

And the guy wrote back: *"If you're rich you don't have to worry about what clients or customers or investors think about you. Or even what friends think about you. So you can say whatever you want."*

By implication it must mean that everyone who thinks they are "poor" is lying to his friends, customers, bosses, etc. This is a horrible way to live, when the ego tightens around you like a straitjacket. Eventually it doesn't end well. All of these friends will backstab you. It's happened to me. Repeatedly.

HONESTY CREATES WEALTH.

Henry Blodget asked me a few months ago, what happened in your writing? Why did it change all of a sudden? I told him, *"I decided to stop lying."*

He gave a nervous laugh (it has to be nervous. Was I lying to him? Was I committing crimes?). He asked, *"what were you lying about?"*

And I was stumped. I don't really know what I was lying about. I had been lying about everything. To everyone. Forever. I couldn't remember telling the truth. I had been following the American religion.

I had basically been broken to the ground. I had 16 out of 17 businesses fail. I survived divorce, losing a home, depression, people dying on me, not seeing my kids for long periods of time, investments fail, I was fired from about eight jobs simultaneously. What was the point? I was just going to write how I saw it. Screw it. It couldn't get worse for me.

For 15 years I've been lying. Ralph (not his real name) used to call me up at 4 in the morning. He was a client of my first business. He needed advice about his job. I couldn't stand him. In fact, at one point he borrowed a lot of money from me he never paid back. And he never paid his bills on time. I had to worry about payroll every month. So at 4 in the morning he'd call for advice and ask: *"Is now an ok time? I couldn't sleep."* And I would always say: *"Of course it is."* When of course, it wasn't. I was lying to him. And it made me hate him even more. And it made me hate myself even more.

You lose yourself when your ego takes charge like that. When you act out of fear, when you are not clear on what your own values are rather than the ones that were imposed onto you.

I've lied quite a bit. To customers, to bosses, to employees, to girlfriends. It doesn't work. It shows less pride in your work, less pride in yourself. It makes people hate you in the long run. It makes you less money. YOU HAVE SEX LESS. YOU DIE EARLIER.

You're better than that. You don't need to blog all your failures and confess all your sins. Let me do that. I have fun with it. Just start small by exercising the honesty muscle.

How to exercise the Honesty Muscle:

Every now and then someone writes me and says "I broke the rules" on the Daily Practice. It is ok to break the rules. It's just a guideline really. But here's an alternative. A simplified version. And it uses the four legs of the Daily Practice to build the Honesty Muscle so you can slowly stop all of your lying. Because don't BS me – you lie also.

Constant self-enquiry is a good way to make sure you are at least being honest with yourself. If you are honest with yourself, you have a reasonable chance at being honest with others.

I can tell you this: so many people are liars: they lie to themselves, they lie to their friends, they lie to their lovers, clients, customers, colleagues, that if you become the one in a thousand that is truly honest, then you will stand out.

And when you stand out you will find success. You will find money. You will find happiness. You will find health (it gives me ulcers to lie because your stomach gets all wrapped up and twisted trying to keep it all straight. You can't digest your food, and your brain starts firing synapses in all the wrong directions)

So... if you ask these core honest questions (see below) to yourself every day then two things will happen:

It will lead to confidence in every aspect of your life. And the more you ask the below questions, the more this honesty will increase. It will lower your center of gravity on the planet. So that wherever you stand, nobody can knock you over.

Your life will be completely different within six months and that difference will be measured in degrees of success.

IMPORTANT: You don't have to answer these questions, "yes!" You just have to be aware when you are saying "No." The more you are aware, ultimately the less "Nos."

PHYSICALLY:

Are you eating healthy? Your body needs food for energy, for health, for cleansing. Everything else drags you down. You can't go from being a persistent snacker to macrobiotic localvore vegan in one day (nor would you want to. I like my fish flown in from Maine!) but make steps to improve what goes in your body.

Are you exercising? Are you keeping clean? Are you sleeping 7-8 hours a night?

Are you doing everything you can do so you don't die an early death from liver or kidney or lung cancer? If you aren't, then you are lying to yourself. If you lie to yourself, you're going to lie to others. It's a horrible spiral down a death trap. Why die earlier and with a lower quality of life than you have to?

This doesn't mean you have to change everything today. Make one change a day. Pick the biggest lie. And make it honest. That's all. But don't BULLSHIT yourself here. It's ok if you're not perfect, if you break the rules here and there. But don't BULLSHIT. Be aware. Be AWAKE. If you aren't the master of your thoughts then you are the slave.

And if you don't want to change anything then at least you're aware of where you are lying. That's not a bad start. But make sure the start has a good End.

EMOTIONALLY:

Are you cheating on wife/partner/friends? Are you being good to your family? To your friends? Not in a way that drains energy from you but are you genuinely giving all you can without doing any draining?

Is anyone being abusive to you in any way? Very important to ask this every day so you can quickly begin the process of dealing with a crappy person.

Do you gossip?

Do you have any big lies going on that are hurting anyone? If so, stop. It's no good for you. Trust me on this. It's too stressful.

Important: Before, during, and after you say anything to anyone think to yourself: am I hurting this person in any way? This goes for employees, employers, customers, clients, friends, family, lovers, haters. This is part of honesty.

Mentally:

Are your ideas good or are you delusional and lying to yourself? The problem with delusion is that almost by definition its hard to know when you are being delusional so it requires constant self-enquiry. Example: are you just flirting with that high school girlfriend on Facebook or are you doing a "dance" here that has intrigue and the real issue is problems in the marriage? Is your business really better than the competition or are their fundamental problems that make your competitor always stand out over you. It's very hard not to lie to yourself in certain situations. Constant self-enquiry as well as following the techniques outlined here will help.

Do you honestly believe that what you are doing at work is helping people? If not, then quit your job or work activity and get a new one. We just had a very hard decade. Everyone's been shot through brain, the heart, the stomach. We all need a little help. Make sure what you do helps a little bit. You might not be able to save a life every day but at least wake up in the morning and ask, *"can I save a life today?"* Who are you asking? Who cares! This is a way to surrender. Not necessarily surrender to a higher power, but just... surrender. To whatever creative force wants to come out and play.

Are you doing your idea lists each day? This helps build up your bullshit detector so you can answer "A" above more carefully.

Are your expectations of yourself too low? Raise them a little each day. IT'S NOT HONEST WITH YOURSELF IF YOU KEEP SAY-ING, "I CAN'T". That's a bullshit line. *"I can't meet that special someone because I'm too busy right now or I don't' live in the right part of the country or I'm too old or I'm too this or too that."* *"I can't get a new job."* *"I can't move right now until I have more money."* Anytime you say *"I can't,"* you're lying to yourself. This is a $15 trillion dollar economy and most of us live in the US. You know what that means? It means "you can." It might take time to make things happen. It might means you have to adjust your life in various ways. But for anything you're saying *"I can't"* about say, "I can."

Again, every day, raise your expectations for yourself a tiny bit high-er. As an example, my expectations of myself might be too low right now. Negotiate into this. Doesn't have to be in one day. Also, use common sense. You can't be eight feet tall. But you can stand up straighter.

SPIRITUALLY:

Everyone has beliefs of some sort. Some people believe if they have more money they will be happier. Some people believe if they go to church every day they will be happier. Maybe either is true or both are true. Every day, ask yourself, are my beliefs really true? Or am I believing them because someone else believes them? Or because I grew up a certain way? It's hard to know if you've been lying to yourself. But it helps to ask.

Here's the simplest spiritual discipline. Every day make a list of new things you are grateful for. And start to only surround yourself with the things you are grateful for. Be grateful only for the things that make you happy. Be honest about what makes you happy and what makes you stressed.

Ultimately that will be your whole life. Being around the people and things you are grateful for makes you honest, because these people will appreciate and reward your honesty the most. These are your friends.

An example for me: I used to read the newspaper every day. But then I realized it was making me tense. The newspapers are the worst liars of all. And I know because I write for them. So I stopped reading them. They can all fire me after reading this. I don't care. Now I'm happier. I replaced the newspaper with books that make me happy. Another example: I used to watch whatever bullshit TV was on between 8 and 10pm. Now I go to sleep earlier. I love sleep. I'm grateful to sleep eight hours and wake up early before the sun rises. I used to go to more dinners than I wanted to. Now I turn down more invitations.

FEAR IS THE ENEMY OF HONESTY. Not lack of wealth. Fear of losing clients. Fear of pissing off family. Fear of going to hell. Fear people won't like you. Fear of being alone. I very much have these fears. But fear never made anyone money or anyone happier or healthier.

LIST THE THINGS YOU ARE AFRAID WILL HAPPEN IF YOU TELL THE TRUTH, even if you just tell the truth to yourself. Are these worthwhile things to be afraid of? If you are going to lose a job by being more honest, should you stay in that job? My guess is you'll be a lot happier in another job. Will you lose your girlfriend if you tell her the truth? My guess is you probably would be happier with someone different if she really would leave you upon hearing the truth. Or maybe you honestly don't know her (or him) as well as you think you do.

I'm afraid all the time. I tell the truth a lot in this blog but of course there's lots of things I leave out. Each day I try to be a little bit more honest with myself in the above four areas. If you are honest in these four areas above then you will have fewer things to fear each day. By November 2010, I had reduced my fear enough I started being honest on this blog. And guess what: my traffic went from 100 visits a day to 10,000 visit's a day.

One caveat in all this: This is not "radical honesty." Don't ever say anything that hurts someone. WHEN YOU'RE HONEST, PEOPLE SENSE IT AND YOUR WORDS HAVE A LOT MORE POWER. I even feel it in the body. When I'm saying something honest I feel as if I'm saying it from my stomach. As if the long stale air that was hanging out there finally gets a chance to burst out with full energy. When I'm lying, I feel as if it's coming from the top of the throat. The last air I inhaled, going right out to escape my lying body. A wisp of breath to accompany my lying words on their journey.

Also beware of self-righteousness, telling an old lie that will only hurt someone today. For example, say that 25 years ago you slept with someone who was dating someone else and now they are happily married. It has been 25 years, they now have three kids and live well, they are happy. Telling the "truth" in this case is not helpful, it will cause unhappiness. This is just a random example, the point is: sharpen your discernment skills. Be clear about your intentions behind using the truth. Use it for good, to get honest with yourself, to find out who you are, to be free, never to hurt.

So you have to be careful with the superpower of honesty. But if you ask the above questions each day, you won't have the opportunity to hurt others. Just be honest with yourself first.

The Smartest Person on The Planet

I was the dumbest person in my graduate school program which is part of the reason why I was thrown out. Stupidity plus immaturity and a willingness to show off both qualities is a bad combination. I thought I was a cowboy. I would show up to final exams having not attended a single class, totally smashed from the night before and not having slept. I had semesters where I failed every single class .

I DID EVERYTHING YOU COULD POSSIBLY DO TO PISS OFF AS MANY PEOPLE AS POSSIBLE IN AS SHORT AMOUNT OF TIME AS POSSIBLE and eventually I got thrown out. Well, I got "asked" to leave. I'm not defending myself. I took bad advantage of a great situation I was in. They paid me a stipend and I used it to do whatever I wanted to do.

Later, when I had to move to the corporate world, I was the stupidest person there as well. Probably because I failed to learn anything in graduate school. I got the job for various reasons that had nothing to do with my abilities and so they didn't know what to do with me. I was so impressed with everyone running around, knowing what to do, knowing how to survive in the big city. I thought to myself, *"these are the real people and I'm faking it."*

On my second day they gave me a computer to put on the Internet. They said, *"you know something about that internet stuff. Get this thing on the internet. But be careful, we keep some email servers on this."* I destroyed that computer so badly it had to be sent back to the manufacturer (Silicon Graphics) and it never came back. I was wearing a suit that didn't fit me. I never wore suits.

It was sunny out. I went outside to use the payphone. No sense making a call like this from my cubicle. I called my girlfriend in Pittsburgh and told her I was about to be fired. She was pretty happy about that. She wanted me back. Which, unfortunately, was my worst nightmare.

Jolie Hunt at Reuters invited me to a dinner a few months ago. I was definitely 100 IQ points lower than anyone there. Tina Brown was sitting next to me. Shawkut Azziz, the former prime minister of Pakistan was across from me. Padma Lakshmi was next to him. I don't even know why I was invited. I concluded during the dinner that I must've done a favor at some point for Jolie but I couldn't remember what it was. The list goes on of the people at this dinner. Everyone had something to say. One of my favorite authors, Ken Auletta, was drilling the former prime minister about how much Pakistan knew about Osama Bin Laden's whereabouts. I was deathly afraid someone would look at me and say, "well, what do you think about all of this? What do you have to say for yourself?"

But after 40 years of being the least smart person in most situations that I've been put in I'VE FINALLY FIGURED OUT HOW TO BE THE SMARTEST PERSON ON THE PLANET.

The Key: Always assume you are the least intelligent person in the room. Always.

Do this in every room, at every dinner, in every situation.

Several things will happen:

YOU'LL LISTEN AND LEARN FROM EVERYONE AROUND YOU. They are all smarter than you. Which means you have a lot to learn from them. Sergey Brin has a trick when he interviews people for Google. He can tell within seconds whether or not he is going to hire someone. If he's NOT going to hire them he knows he still has to suffer through another twenty minutes with them. So he always makes it a point to learn at least one thing from them so it's not a total waste of time. I do this with every person I meet ever. Because I happen to know a secret about them: they are smarter than me.

This is not a false humility. I haven't been very good at school (which is probably why I write so many articles about why college is bad). And I haven't made a billion dollars despite the opportunities I've had. I've made many many stupid mistakes that I have a hard time forgiving myself for. I could've saved lives and instead I squandered them. I got good at squandering.

The good thing I have going for me is that I LOOK smart. I have curly hair and glasses. And I'm Jewish and people stereotype all of the above. Oh, and I'm good at chess. Which people also equate with intelligence but this isn't true.

WHEN YOU'RE DONE LISTENING, LISTEN TO THE SILENCE. Trust me, people never finish talking. Once you've learned something from someone and they are done talking, then skip your turn to talk and let them talk again. They'll do it. Not because of arrogance. It's because they have more to teach you. So listen some more.

NOW WHEN THEY ARE DONE TALKING, ASK AT LEAST ONE QUESTION. They'll do A and B again. You'll learn more. As I'm writing this it almost feels like I'm making fun of the people I'm listening to. But that couldn't be further from the truth.

I'LL GIVE YOU A QUICK EXAMPLE. I'm in a computer lab right now. Some guy, 31 years old, was just sitting at the computer next to me, looking for apartment rentals in Houston. I asked him why he's moving to Houston. He just took a job at ExxonMobil. I THOUGHT THE US HAD RUN OUT OF OIL, I said to him, immediately underlining my stupidity. He then explained to me how Texas has more oil than Saudi Arabia with all the new techniques and technologies and fracking, etc. I thought "fracking" was from Battlestar Galactica. He explained the whole thing to me. He drew diagrams of how the drills work. Of how oil and gas flows out of the rocks. I then googled it after he left to learn more and make sure I understood. I don't know if Texas has more oil than Saudi Arabia but I certainly learned a lot more than I knew two hours ago.

Intelligence compounds exponentially. It's the "network effect". In a system (like the Internet) with the network effect, the more people that use it, the value of the entire network goes up exponentially. Which is why the value and profit of companies like Facebook and Zynga have gone up so fast compared with companies in prior generations. And why the entire Internet exploded upwards like it did. But in the case of intelligence, the "network" is the neurons in your brain. Learn new things and new neurons wake up and start firing synapses with each other, increasing exponentially the "value" (intelligence) of the "network" (your brain).

So try this: be the least intelligent person at every meeting and gathering. You're a spy, gathering all the intel you can. Unlike everyone else at the meeting, you are guaranteed to learn something (because everything people say is something you don't know, almost by definition). Because of the compounding effect, at some point, you will be the smartest.

Humility. At the very least, assuming you are smart, you will be able to practice and cultivate a healthy humility, which is never bad.

But, you might ask: shouldn't one exude confidence and demonstrate intelligence so people are impressed?

Answer: No. People will forget you. Not everyone. But most. Because that's what people do. They move onto the next thing. But if you consciously cultivate humility and learn from everyone you meet, you will be the one who will never forget them. And, before long, you'll be the smartest person on the planet. And when the aliens land and say, "we are going to talk to your leader", everyone around you will be surprised when the aliens go straight to you.

Light Your Creativity on Fire

I felt so ashamed. I had just lost my apartment in the city. I had no jobs. No prospects for jobs. No money. A few years earlier I had millions and then I had nothing. So I sold my apartment, scraped together some cash, and moved 70 miles north of the city. It was in the middle of a blizzard. I was scared of my neighbors.

I couldn't get out of bed I was so depressed. I gained twenty pounds because I never moved my body. There was blizzard after blizzard. I didn't go into the city at all, not even to attend the closing of my hated apartment, which took me almost two years to sell (at almost 50% of the price I originally listed at). I had no phone. Didn't need one. I didn't feel like I would have any skills for a job and it was a recession anyway. I was really scared because my dad's career had basically ended in a similar way and then fizzled out from depression. The same thing was going to happen to me, I was sure of it.

I got an email the other day. Someone asked me, *"when you are totally out of luck and feeling incredibly down, how do you spark that creativity up so you can get going again?"*

We're all creative people. Unless we're just going to disappear and die, you have to spark it up again at some point. And recession and politics doesn't matter. We're in a $15 trillion economy. There's $3 trillion in cash lying in the bank. There's six million private businesses. So once you're creative again there's no reason you can't make money. Lots of it. I don't care what the debt ceiling did today or what imaginary monster "downgraded" some other imaginary monster. None of that matters for creative people. None of that matters for you and me.

NINE STEPS TO GET MORE CREATIVE RIGHT NOW

- Turn Upside Down. Not literally. But take any topic people hold dear. Turn it upside down. Pick a topic that people hold so dear it's like a religion, just pick up one from the chapter on the American religion. Take education for example. Start thinking every day of 10 new ways people can get educated.

- KHAN ACADEMY (a website for teaching mathematics) is doing pretty good. Is he the only guy out there who can do something like that? Of course not. Advertising is another area. Publishing is another area. Turn it all upside down.

- REAL ESTATE is another area that can still be turned upside down. Airbnb is only the start. Zillow is only the start. There's a million ways. Take any topic that is practically a religious topic. Say out loud, "the way the world does this right now is bull-shit" and start thinking "why" and "how" to make it better. You're not going to solve all the world's problems right here. This is all to just start off exercising the creativity muscles. You need to start firing those neurons or axons or whatever again. But you never know, sometimes if you exercise enough, you can actually become a professional piano mover.

- LIST OPTIONS. In chess, the first thing a grandmaster does when it's his turn is not look deeply down one variation but rather take a step back and list all possible option moves.

Take a pad (my favorite choice: the waiter's pad) and start listing options. I still do this all the time. Since it's your own private pad your options can be as insane as possible. Who cares? It's your pad!

I made a list of options the other day. Even if I don't intend to do any of these it's always helpful to list the possibilities for yourself. To list your options:

- Start a fund (this led to another list of types of funds, types of investors, etc).

- Start another online business (and then this led to another list).

- Write a book about "the American Religion" (this led to me doing a list of chapters).

- Write a novel (working on it today).

- Try being a standup comedian just once.

- Get more speaking gigs.

- Create a "Dear Abby" column on the blog, now happening through Twitter.

- Pitch a TV show (blech!).

- Become a world famous painter (why not?)

And so on. These were the least embarrassing that is why I list them here.

And for every option you list, that creates new potential lists of options.

When I write "pitch a TV show" that means I now have to make a list of all the possible options there. The more sub-lists you write, the closer you get to execution.

Again, this is not supposed to lead to anything (yet) but just as exercises to kickstart the creativity. This also assumes you are getting the rest of your life together: The Daily Practice plus Avoiding Crappy People.

COMBINE IDEAS. Let's say there are 10,000 possible things you can be interested in. That means there's over 100,000,000 ways to combine any two ideas to make a new idea. When I first met Claudia (an Argentinian fully dedicated with yoga) I instantly told her, *"you should create Tango Yoga!"* Take Tango moves, combine them with Yoga moves, write a book, take photos of beautiful tango dancers doing yoga poses, give classes, do a DVD, etc. Only problem is, she's the only Argentinian on the planet who doesn't know how to tango.

But that's just an example. When I started Stockpickr I took my two main interests at the time: making websites, and daytrading, and combined them into one website. BAM!

So do it! List all the things you've ever been interested in in your life. See which ones you can combine. Again, we're just doing this for fun. No pressures. I'm IMing one guy right now as I type this: he's interested in both the bible and being an entrepreneur. How about a book? "The 10 Best Entrepreneurs in the Bible"! BAM! Is it a good idea? Who knows? But if he does it I bet he can make a living getting speaking gigs about it. And he can self-publish using the techniques I explained on a previous chapter and not wait a year for some clueless publisher to figure out how to print up his book.

NEW TECHNOLOGY. When the iPad came out, everyone should've been listing the multiple businesses that would be created off of that ecosystem. Now that we have Google+ I know several people already brainstorming the various businesses that can be created off of that. And do you think "location-based" is done? Do you think it was just a fad? We are not even singing the National Anthem on that one yet. Inning number one is still years away. Start thinking man! And show me the idea before you show it to anyone else.

Start reading about every new technology you can find. You don't need to be a nuclear rocket scientist to make use of new technologies. That's what third-world outsourcers are for. You're the idea guy! The cowboy on the frontier! There's technology now that can take your brainscan and tell you what letter you were thinking of. When are we going to have the "wiki-chip" that links Wikipedia to my brain? Chop-chop! Let's do it.

One word on pitching ideas:

Don't tell me your whole life story. Describe your product in two lines, otherwise it is not worth anyone's time. Show me that you thought it through, give me the execution plan, step by step. Don't bullshit me. Don't ask for money before we even know it is a good idea. Get real, be consice, respect time.

CONNECT PEOPLE. Why is LinkedIn so successful? Because it connects people. LinkedIn is worth billions. You don't need to be worth that much. How about you become a mini-LinkedIn today? Find 5 sets of two people you can connect. It's just like combining ideas only now you are combining people.

You don't need any benefit from it. If you can think of two people who can help each other and you put them together then the universe will take care of your benefit. You don't have to spend one ounce of energy thinking about it. Just be creative about who you can put together. Ok, GO!

I've gone to about four dinners in the past few months where the entire purpose of the dinners was to throw people together. I've gotten insulted, brutalized, made fun of, laughed at by Prime Ministers, ignored by supermodels, scoffed at by presidential candidates, but it's been a great experience for someone as anti-social as me. And it's strengthened my rolodex of people who I can introduce to each other. Become a connector.

MAKE SOMETHING. I don't know how to paint, sculpt, collage, photograph, nothing. So those areas of my brain are completely dormant and atrophied. It would probably help every area of my creativity, including my business creativity and writing creativity if I just take out the watercolors my kids use and paint something. Or take a bunch of women's fashion magazines and make a collage. It would take my mind off any anxieties I have, and get me focused on some creative time while at the same time I would be riding a steep learning curve.

So I asked my kids to give me a lesson on how to draw manga comic book characters. They were great teachers, I got to spend quality time with them, I sparked my creativity in an area I never thought of, and I made "stuff" (I have to call it that since I'm not sure they would approve of me calling it "manga").

LEAVE. You heard me. Go. Get away. Leave your house. Get in the car and drive a few hours away. Call in sick at work. Go someplace you've never been before. Turn your mind off for a day. Find an obscure museum you can visit.

In 2004 I got a letter from the IRS. I got scared. At first I panicked. But then once the situation started to calm down I did the only thing I could do – I left. I went to an ashram sort of place for a long weekend in the middle of nowhere. I didn't speak at all for three days. I ate good food. I exercised, meditated, sat at the table where nobody spoke, and kept to myself. By the time I got back I was ready to start my next business and I did, and it worked.

You can't leave all the time. But one afternoon every two or three weeks take an "art day" for yourself. Leave and don't look back. Have fun.

Virtually Leave. Sometimes when I'm thinking about what to write about I start checking out websites that I know do a good job curating creativity. Inevitably it will have me start thinking. Here are some of my favorites:

- Boingboing.net

- Thebrowser.com

- Extragoodshit.phlap.net (note: not safe for work. This site is run by an 80 year old guy who is an awesome curator of creativity. BUT, he intermixes the great sites with his favorite artistic porn pictures. He can do without those but I'm sure they drive traffic.)

- Brainpickings.org

- Claudiayoga.com (My wife, of course, has the best website of all!)

There's about 1000 others. They get the juices flowing in my brain sometimes. Usually I try to write by reading first and getting that to inspire me. I'll read a writer with a strong autobiographical voice. If that doesn't get me going I'll switch to a spiritual text. If that doesn't get me going, I start hitting the above sites.

Seek help. Sometimes you really are down and out. Sometimes you really can't get out of bed. Sometimes life has beaten down on you or me or whoever a little too much. That's ok also. You can't just go to a museum and suddenly your brain is on fire with ideas. Every now and then you need a little bit of extra love and attention. Don't ignore the possibility that you might need a doctor to talk, to medicate, to listen, and just work through things while you are going through a tough period.

Eventually, in 2002, after my depressive exile from NYC, after all the blizzards, and the silence, and the anxiety of wondering if I was ever going to get off the floor again, I found my creative voice. But it took all of the above. It took the Daily Practice. It took the various posts I mention below. Most of all, it took me getting out of bed and telling myself that I wanted to live again.

I'm still alive.

Be Alive

One guy I worked closely with in the Internet boom killed himself about a year ago. His father had died recently and he was very close to his father. My friend had a heart condition plus various cancers that kept coming back. He had been fired from AOL in some sort of scandal, and the company we had worked together at, back in 1999, had gone bankrupt. He was overweight, had no girlfriend, had a speech impediment, and he was constantly sweating due to his various illnesses.

I was talking about him at a dinner with friends. We were all saying what a great guy he was. Because he truly was a great guy. When you go through so much sorrow you know that it makes no sense to be mean or cruel to the people around you. Finally, though, it occurred to all of my friends that I was the only one at the table who didn't know he was dead. *"Wait a sec,"* said one of the people at dinner, *"you don't know?"*

"Know what?"

And the table went silent. Nobody wanted to say. An awful secret had been served at the table and I was the only one not feasting on the dish. Instead someone gave me a URL and I went to it later and it was a tribute page to my friend. I've had 100 breakfasts with the guy and I didn't know and it made me wonder what his last thoughts were. The last time I heard from him he had sent me a random email in 2005 that said, *"James! Is this email address really for you?"* And, true to my form, I never responded. I meant to respond. But I put it off. Then never did.

Nobody wants to die. But it's hard to go from wanting to die to suddenly being cheered up. If you say, *"I want to die"* and everyone else says, *"Oh, cheer up, there's so much to live for"* that's sometimes a hard thing to hear. It's not like you're going to suddenly say: *"You know what? You are totally right. I'm cheered up now!"*

Try this instead. Just think a little deeper. When you get that feeling ask yourself, *"What is it inside of me that really wants to die?"*

Do you really want your heart to stop beating? I hardly ever think of the mechanics of my heart. Why would I suddenly want it to stop beating? I don't even know what side of my chest my heart is on.

So what do you really want to die?

The times when I've thought it, what I really wanted (when I think about it in retrospect):

- I wanted death to the horrible feeling that so-and-so didn't return my affections the way I wanted her to (maybe she didn't call back, was with another guy, didn't respond to emails, didn't tell me she loved me, etc)

- I wanted death to the fear that put it'self-right in my gut that I was going to go broke. A constant fear that has recurred again and again in my life.

- I wanted death to the fear that I was going to lose my house (when I still bought into the amerian religion concept that owning a home was like owning a life). Or death to the pain I felt upon losing a house. That pain sitting in my head and stomach which buried me underneath so many failures one after the other that I thought I could never climb out of the coffin / grave they buried me in.

- I wanted the death of the utter sorrow I felt when my dad died.

- I wanted death to the fear the IRS was going to put me in jail (unfounded, but who knew?)

- I wanted the death of the ongoing anticipation of whether or not I was going to sell a company before it went out of business.

- I wanted the death of the horrible feeling in my stomach when a stock I owned a lot of was moving against me and I had clients that depended on me.

- I wanted death to the sadness that my kids, whom I love, would grow up not knowing me in the way I originally thought they would know me (because divorce changes the way, forever, you interact with your kids)

- I wanted the death of the feeling of inadequacy I felt upon losing a chess tournament or money at a poker session or not getting a novel published again and again and again.

- I wanted the death of the anger I felt towards family members who I felt had horribly wronged me. Or the obsession that place in your head when you are dealing with crappy people. I would want the death of that obsession.

And on and on. So many different times I've thought it – *"I want to die."* Sometimes I meant it, sometimes I didn't. But when I look back on it, never did I really want my heart to stop beating. I just wanted the death of these various emotions that were hurting me not just emotionally but physically.

I wanted the death of my lack of control over a world that is furious, and chaotic and beautiful and messy.

And all of those things did die eventually. How small they are in the rear view mirror. And a little bit of me died with each one of them.

But I'm still alive.

Be a Human

A lot of anonymous people get angry on message boards. VERY angry. And to what purpose? Will they be happier by being so angry? Will they feel they've accomplished something by anonymously cursing someone out? Will life be more fulfilled for them?

But it got me to wonder about the psychology of people who take valuable time out of their day to write some of these ugly and anonymous things. Not just about me but about anyone.

In general people get angry at me because I say in various ways that the world is not falling apart. That we're not all going to die at the hands of some obscure European debt crisis or whatever the latest crisis of the week is in the media.

Many people feel very strongly against some of my opinions. One woman wrote an article "James Altucher is an idiot" and then when she was getting zero views she emailed me the article so she'd have at least one view. To guarantee one view you can email me an article titled "James Altucher is an idiot" and I am sure to read it at the very least out of curiosity.

Other people replied on various message boards about what a F****ng loser I was, etc etc.

They seem to care more about my opinions than I do.

If my daughter comes to me and says, *"I'm sad because I'd like to have more friends"* then I would care about that. If my wife were sick I'd care about that. If I was sick I would VERY much care about that. I'm selfish. I'd care about my own sickness more than I'd care about my daughter's ability to make friends. I also care if I am writing interesting things. Or if I'm reading books that will make me a better writer. Of if I'm winning more at chess now that I'm taking chess lessons. I care about these things. If people write to me and ask for advice, I care a lot about the advice I give. But about the rest of the world, I don't care at all. How big can one head be?

I don't blame anyone for being angry at me. But I can tell you exactly why they were angry.

Here's why:

- Their fathers or mothers didn't love them.

- Other kids beat on them

- Girls (or guys) didn't like them or called them names.

- Their friends backstabbed them.

So now they want to do the same to other people. So rather than working at their jobs they go from article to article and whatever message boards they can, then anonymously spew their hate.

Many of these people would like to kill themselves. I hate to say it but it's true. I feel bad for them. How do I know they would like to kill themselves? How can I possibly be so psychic as to know this, particularly since in most cases they are anonymous so I don't even know what sex, age, race, religion, location, they are.

I know this because they want the world to end. They keep blaming their problems on how bad the world is. How the world is falling apart. How we *"borrowed too much"* or how *"the United States is going to fail"* or how *"Europe is going to take us down"* or how *"China is going to take over the world."* It's an easy excuse so they don't have to blame themselves on their own failures. They can blame me instead because I don't think *"China is going to take over the world."*

My blog has become a mini laboratory of sorts. I see the kind of people who react on my blog. I've seen anonymous people throw racial epithets. I've seen friends come out of nowhere and trash me. I've had all sorts of hate mail and hate comments. And out of the thousands I've gotten (although, thankfully, a lot more positive feedback than negative feedback by about a 10:1 ratio) I've been able to truly see the concept of "projection" at work.

I used to think it was psychotherapeutic BS. I'd say to a girlfriend, *"you're being cruel to me,"* and she would respond, *"you are projecting."*

But now I see, it's true. When people are beaten as a kid, they hate themselves. But they don't look in the mirror and say, *"I hate you."* They go to you and say, *"I hate you."* And they do it in all sorts of ways that don't make any sense to you.

Why don't they make sense to you? Because they are projecting. Because it's their problem. How would you know they were beaten as a kid? You can't. And what's worse now is that the world used to be safe for them. They didn't have to take their hate out on anyone. Now the world is different.

The world is manic-depressive. Right now, and maybe for the past decade, the world has been in the depressive cycle. The Internet bust, 9/11, Enron corruption, the financial crisis, the housing crisis, Europe crisis, unemployment. I get it. It's been a hard decade. It's been a hard decade for me also. Before that it was in the manic cycle.

Animals ebb and flow with the world's cycles. Humans rise above it and create their own cycles. I don't know if I'm a human or an animal (I know, humans are a subset of animals, but I'm making a point). I'm a little bit of both. I hate to see the world depressed so I try to do things (go on TV, write articles, whatever) to convince people the world is not over. But it's pretty pointless. People believe what they will because of that severe beating they had when they were nine that they could never shake themselves from.

How to be Human?

DO THE DAILY PRACTICE. It's the only way I've ever been able to rise above animal and be human. I've lied, cheated, stolen, failed again and again. I've failed not only myself but all the people around me. I've felt suicidal. I've tried every trick, medication, therapy, meditation, etc.

Finally it all stopped when I decided to focus on my insides instead of the outside. That's how you train your body and mind to get over the beatings as a kid, the humiliation you've suffered, the lack of love you might've had to deal with. In my opinion (take it for what it's worth), it's the only way.

DON'T ENGAGE WITH CRAPPY PEOPLE. The woman who emailed me her fabulous article: "James Altucher is an Idiot" – I actually responded to her email. I didn't even follow my own advice. Then, finally, I stopped responding to her on her four responses to me. It's hard to follow good advice. If everyone followed good advice we'd all be superheroes and be flying around and using our x-ray vision to see naked people everywhere. I wish I followed my own advice every day. But it's hard. Sometimes you have to modify it to fit your own needs and circumstances. Sometimes you have to modify every day.

BE CREATIVE EVERY DAY. You can use these tips. Creativity connects more and more of the neurons in your brain to each other. Neurons that animals never connect up. If you are too busy with work, child raising, business-starting, etc don't use that as an excuse. You can be creative in little, tiny ways. Make your kids laugh. Do something the exact opposite of what you would normally do at work. Try standing on your head at the busstop. Whatever.

THE LAST THREE ITEMS ARE THE MOST IMPORTANT. If you do those then the first two come naturally. If the above three items are too hard then modify them to suit your own purposes. For instance, if you can't meditate every day (I can't) then at least when you wake up say to the sky "what the hell do you want me to do today? I'm yours!" In other words, be gentle, humble, and surrender.

FIGHT THE FEAR. Fear is a daily part of my life. I'm tired of it. I'm tired of the fight. Using the technique described in the chapter above I've been able to get a grip on it. And what is the result? It means I can pursue other things. I can pursue building a business. I can pursue making money. I can engage in more spiritual pursuit's or creative pursuit's (like this book, for instance). Fear will make you sick, kill you, slow you down, and prevent you from doing the things you need to do in this short life we have.

USE THE POWER OF NEGATIVE THINKING. This applies not only to anger and fear but to all of the ways we've been brainwashed in our lives. Think in terms of opposites. Always consider things, particularly the things that people are willing to die for, in terms of a 360 degree viewpoint. Nobody is out there "defending your way of life". Only you can do that. But first you have to figure out what your way of life is. Find out what it is you want without listening to the Mega Zombie Recruitment Machine.

DON'T BE AN ANIMAL ANYMORE. Planet of the Apes isn't coming true. You don't have to live in the world of Zombieland or "I, Robot". Be nice to other people. Become a human. Become more than human. Open your eyes and see for yourself.

Why?

Because freedom at least for me, is a very different concept than I was initially brainwashed into believing. Freedom is a feeling, a sensation that we experience when we know we are coming from wisdom, power, discernment, peace.

Freedom happens when we feel our feet on the ground and observe people around us without any fear, When we feel solid enough to quit our jobs if it is not serving the purpose of our spirit, when we can distinguish that real roots are the ones we grow towards our own personal beliefs rather than measured by how deep the white picked fence goes into the yard.

Because seeing is connecting with our internal creativity and waking up saying "YES" I get another day to live and I am loving what I do. I am BEING who I am, I am following the stellar configuration that created the special, unique, individual cirumstances that I recognize aas myself. Because there is nobody in the planet like me.

Seeing is realizing that all the wealth and success in the world is ours for the taking once we've build the foundations within, the true freedom that lets us see the reality and the myths around us for what they are.

It is questioning every thing we do and the intentions behind them

It is realizing that sometimes our intentions have a lot of strings attached and that not being honest is expensive. Very expensive.

These techniques, these ideas, I've learned the hard way. I've succeeded on traditional terms. I've failed on very traditional terms. I've been brainwashed by the Zombie Recruitment Machine. But I've also used the techniques in this book to now create success for myself. Nothing I suggest in this book is without decades of exploration and experimentation. Don't take my word for it.

Now is the time for you to take your own journey. To SEE the world. To figure out what you truly want, find success, wealth, freedom, happiness, and live the life you always knew you were meant to live. Enjoy.

Made in the USA
Lexington, KY
27 September 2011